MW00736588

THE RETREAT FROM ORGANIZATION

THE RETREAT FROM ORGANIZATION

U.S. Feminism Reconceptualized

ELISABETH ARMSTRONG

STATE UNIVERSITY OF NEW YORK PRESS

Published by
STATE UNIVERSITY OF NEW YORK PRESS
ALBANY

© 2002 State University of New York

All rights reserved

Printed in the United States of America

No part of this book may be used or reproduced in any manner whatsoever without written permission. No part of this book may be stored in a retrieval system or transmitted in any form or by any means including electronic, electrostatic, magnetic tape, mechanical, photocopying, recording, or otherwise without the prior permission in writing of the publisher.

For information, address
State University of New York Press
90 State Street, Suite 700, Albany, NY 12207

Production, Laurie Searl
Marketing, Jennifer Giovani-Giovani

Library of Congress Cataloging-in-Publication Data

Armstrong, Elisabeth, 1967–
    The retreat from organization: U.S. feminism reconceptualized/Elisabeth Armstrong.
      p. cm.
    Includes bibliographical references and index.
    ISBN 0-7914-5215-8 (alk. paper)—ISBN 0-7914-5216-6 (pbk.: alk. paper)
      1. Feminism—United States. 2. Feminist therory—United States. I. Title.

HQ1421 .A75 2002
305.42′0973—dc21
                                                    2001048345

10   9   8   7   6   5   4   3   2   1

CONTENTS

ACKNOWLEDGMENTS

The libraries, archives, and personal collections of labor, Left, women's, and civil rights movements in the sixties and seventies provided invaluable and often surprising materials about theories of organizing women. I would like to thank the following archivists for their generosity with their time and knowledge: Jane E. Hodes from the Niebyl-Proctor Marxist Library for Social Research, Mary Licht from the Reference Center for Marxist Studies, Anne E. Champagne from the Women's Collection of Northwestern University Library, Hilary Diamond from the Holt Labor Library, Ernie Haberkern from the Center for Socialist History, Kathleen Nuffer from the Sophia Smith Collection at Smith College, and Gary Lundell from the Archives Division of the University of Washington Library.

Early incarnations of this book showed up in classes I taught at Brown University and in subsequent courses at Trinity College and Wesleyan University. I want to thank the students in these classes who actively engaged with strange, partially digested archival materials and challenged how we think of women's activism. To all the rabble rousers at Brown University, I salute your independence of spirit and the strength of your will to fight for justice. In particular, for their inspiration and support I would like to thank my comrades Leyla Mei, Libero Della Piana, Amie Fishman, Alisa Gallo, Padma Rajagopalan, Rafi Brown, Greg Smith, Lihbin Shao, Larry Yu, Greg Nammacher, Cassy Stubbs, Ray Neiryncks, Becky Smith, and the many others who refuse to say "uncle." I would like to honor here the courage and integrity of another activist from this rich seam of subversives, Kathy DeLeon. She will not be forgotten.

A wealth of support and sustenance springs from so many colleagues, friends, and family that this book is truly a collective enterprise. Warmest thanks especially to Vrinda Narain, Kasturi Ray, Gautam Premnath, Kaleem Siddiqi, Amit Bose, Sorayya Khan, Jennifer Campbell, Zaira Rivera-Casellas, Sangeeta Kamat, Biju Mathew, Edmund Campos, Sunaina Maira, Ellen Rooney, Mari Jo Buhle, Lewis Gordon, Joan Hedricks, Barbara Sicherman, Sudhir Venkatesh, Kaichen Locke, Jane Gordon, Emma Fair, Brian Steinbeck, Joelle Fishman, Marilyn Filley, Arabella Holzbog, and Erin Keesey, who freely shared a patient ear and their myriad talents. Here's to new adventures with my colleagues at Smith, Susan Van Dyne, Marilyn Schuster, Gwendolyn Mink, Ann Fergeson, and many others. For unflagging comic relief and energy to organize, I send my love out to Young Communist League's young people in Hartford who keep the car's sound system in high gear. My family has given fiercely loyal support throughout all of my adventures. I thank my parents Margaret and Peter, my sister Katharine, and my brother Philip. To my mother-in-law, Soni Prashad, and my late father-in-law, Pran Prashad, I send cross-oceanic thanks. For inspiration and insight, I can only marvel at the revolutionary generosity of my aunts Brinda Karat and Radhika Roy. Most of all I thank Vijay Prashad for a vibrant partnership that extends far beyond shared tasks, experiences, or beliefs. Together we have learned to celebrate the nuances of struggle and the productivity of organization. Finally, to Zalia Maya, whose effortless joy hastened the completion of this book.

The Feminist Critique

The second wave women's movement in the United States has reached an age of memory; it is now old enough to be forgotten, distorted, or both simultaneously.[1] But hard-won lessons of determined resistance linger. Activists and fellow travelers have kept their watch, and an influx of books about second wave feminism continues to make history of their stories. Autobiographical memoirs by Karla Jay of Radicalesbians and Susan Brownmiller of New York Radical Women remind us of these activists' daily political lives, reactions, and feelings.[2] Biographies about Betty Friedan and Germaine Greer suggest possible feminist political futures.[3] Collections like *The Feminist Memoir Project* gather the present assessments of second wave feminist activists, many of whom are better known by other activists than by a mass-media audience.[4] These memories exist alongside recent anthologies of past writings, such as Alma Garcia's edited collection entitled *Chicana Feminist Thought: The Basic Historical Writings,* and histories that create narratives from the chaotic amalgam of dreams and hard work sometimes called "the women's movement."[5] Books about, by, and for the women's movement are nothing new, as they build canons, argue for particular trajectories, and recruit and educate new participants. But these more recent texts emerge alongside another discourse, that of a third wave of feminism, a movement for younger women, markedly different in ideas and context.[6] The stakes have shifted, since these memories now consolidate and reassess a movement past in relation to a movement future.[7]

These books are all histories inasmuch as they piece together the past, but they are also part of a collective effort, what Frigga Haug calls "memory-work."[8] As a methodology, memory-work is twofold: the subject of memory-work is also its object, and the analysis of memories should be a collective process. In the first aspect of memory-work, the line between the subject and object of study blurs.[9] This is as true of Ruth Rosen's large-canvas history, *The World Split Open,* as it is of Brownmiller's account giving her side of the story, *In Our Time: Memoir of a Revolution.* As participants, observers, and social scientists, these authors must concede objectivity, but also authenticity. Even the painstaking detail of Rosen's history does not pretend to account for every nuance or experience in the second wave women's movement. Rosen celebrates the necessary incompleteness of her undertaking: "There were many stories; there are many memories. I hope there will be many more histories."[10] Brownmiller characterizes her story as "partisan," but she draws on numerous sources to give shape, even meaning, to her own recollections.[11] In history and memoir, writers like Rosen and Brownmiller overlap the personal and political to admit 'feminism' as their subject/object of study. Memory as empirical data adapts to its investigator while it changes her, a process only heightened by remembering a collective movement.

Haug concentrates on the empirical data of personal memory to understand how "individuals construct themselves into existing structures."[12] Recent books about the women's movement often center on individuals in and around feminist politics. But this ostensible focus allows another construction and intervention to enter as if by allegory: the radical movements of feminism. The insertion of the women's movement into social structures and relations seems more obvious, perhaps, or more conscious than that of an individual. But feminism and the women's movement as objects of study are notoriously hard to grasp, hard to pin down to a particular definition, formation, or site. To speak of the women's movement demands a jump from singular to plural and back again. These personal/historical memories visualize a women's movement, unitary only in the moment of its evocation. As soon as the story of feminism begins, the movement multiplies, intersects, and contradicts itself. The collectivity of feminism changes not only with each perspective, but also as it projects infinite possibilities. However, these destabilizing contingencies within the subject/object, singular/plural feminism also grant the possibility to theorize the movement on its own terms, that is, to create analytic categories through memory.

Part of a very public arena, these books challenge all readers to enter the construction and analysis of second wave feminist pasts, even if we were too young to remember them ourselves. In their introductions and prefaces, authors state their intentions clearly: they write so no one must forget. Karla Jay characterizes the traffic of contorted memories today:

> Whether I'm talking to the urban cool or to budding activists on a rural college campus, I find that their assumptions about this history are often framed by comedians, pundits, and other forms of popular media that aim for a quick punchline rather than complex truths. Those interested in women's studies ask: "Did feminists have sex? Camille Paglia says you didn't."[13]

Jay talks about the investment in simplified memories, ones that not only pack a punch but also wipe clean any nuanced discussions about the movement's contradictory and complex aspects. Jay makes larger questions possible, such as, was it a movement at all? What makes a movement? Does a movement need leaders? If not, what new relations of power take their place? Books like Jay's generously add to a memory bank, one open to a collective process of analysis that asks what happened, what techniques worked, what experiments failed, and how we conceive the women's movement today. This memory-work resonates beyond the mere recitation of the past to imagined futures.

The flaws in American feminism have received extensive coverage in mainstream and academic writings. Unfortunately, criticisms of social, political, and economic relations generated by feminist analyses have not been aired so generously. This manuscript focuses on critiques of feminism in relation to feminism as a politically interested grouping that engenders theory and politics.[14] I ask how feminism links theory to politics, and to whom and what feminism must be held accountable. Most importantly, I sample a wide range of political movements and groups from the mid-sixties to the present, to uncover their answers and their conceptual beginnings around feminism. This historical breadth allows a range of visions about feminism to emerge, from a pressure group within radical politics to an interlocking piece of a larger revolutionary movement to a code of ethics to a chosen identity.[15] Impressive works by Shane Phelan, Nan Hunter, and Lisa Duggan have begun to theorize feminist, lesbian, and queer politics in books and articles that refuse to concede any ground to the misleading theory/politics dichotomy.[16] In this spirit, I argue that to debate feminism in an era of globalized multinational capitalism, our overwhelming focus on the subjects(s) of feminism is too narrow. To ignore organizational questions of feminisn elides how feminism as a collective movement proposes to change structural forces that bind the exploitation of women workers around the world in differential, but unavoidably linked relations of production. Through a renewed questioning of feminism's organizational mechanisms and presumptions, I argue, our memory work can expand our conceptual lens from the subject(s) of feminism toward feminism as an imagined, yet wholly real construct of future political transformation.[17]

This book develops two key terms to discuss feminism. I elaborate the categories 'organization' and 'struggle' in relation to feminist writings of the second wave women's movement in the United States, and draw on their earlier articulation by such marxists as Rosa Luxemburg, Georg Lukács, and Vladimir Lenin. But this study does not pursue how these concepts developed historically, why they developed, or even what contexts they reflect. Instead it asks, What is feminist critique? and discovers the answer in the interaction of these two terms. In this sense, organization is a concept that operates on multiple levels. First, organization is a theoretical category of analysis that nonetheless mediates theory and practice. In chapter 1, I argue that organization helps us to conceptualize feminism simultaneously through its theories and its practices. Second, organization provides the basis for a methodological shift in our discussions about feminism. In chapter 2, I show how an organizational analysis of pluralism in antiracist feminism reveals the weaknesses of feminism conceived primarily through its subject. Third, *political* organization represents an object, the formalization of disparate struggles into a structure. In chapter 3, I argue against antiorganizational theories of feminism that continue to connect their visions for a nonhierarchical feminism to their rejection of formal organization. Finally, political organization and its relationship to struggle are important sites for debates about feminism. In chapters 4 and 5, I examine three central organizational issues for feminism: group interconnections (whether alliances, coalitions, or less formal collaborations), representation, and leadership. The debates in each chapter, around feminist racism, non-hierarchical feminist structures, and cross-movement coalitions do not begin to encompass the full range of debates about organization in the second wave women's movement. The retreat of organization, then, marks a waning presence of explicit questions about feminism as a collective movement. But organizational concerns have not fully disappeared, even in the most dedicated poststructualist theories of feminist politics, though its traces are more difficult to discern. Class, like race, and nationality become attributes of individual women. Elitism, racism, national chauvinism and ethnocentricism become individual problems, though ones experienced and fought on a larger scale. This difference between organizational and individual configurations of struggle may seem subtle or abstract at best, and irrelevant at worst. For the emergence of third wave feminisms, however, the retreat of organization has improvished our sense of the past and the future. What disturbs me about this gradual erasure is the consequent loss of the language to discuss feminism as a collective entity, albeit an ever-changing one, and the means to envision even as we enact new forms of feminist politices.

Chapter 1 defines organization as an extension of the concerns about political economy. I build on the insights of Nancy Fraser's critique of feminist impasses and atomization and her call for reinvigorated analyses of political economy.[18] But I argue that political economy's analytical emphasis on the social totality is not enough to combat the discontinuities among and distances between feminisms. Instead, I elaborate another definition of political economy based on earlier writings about revolution in the second wave women's movement. Feminism as a movement must not merely resuscitate its commitment to the redistribution of wealth, as Fraser argues, but must make conscious the theories of organization that inform its political values. That is, feminists need a substantive debate about their ideals and goals as well as about their tactics and strategies.[19] Earlier articulations of political economy did not rest on any feminist certainties: not of a movement, nor of women or politics. These writings struggle to envision revolution in relation to gender and women. In the process, they elaborate the dynamic relationship between theory and practice. They illustrate organization as Lukács defines the term—as the mediation between theory and practice. They debate the effects of this organizational analysis of feminism as a political vision of social transformation and as a movement embodying its ideals. Ideals, social totality, strategies, and tactics create feminist practices, even as they are produced by an emerging movement.

In chapter 2, I discuss the methodological insights of an organizational analysis. This chapter details the weaknesses of pluralism as a discursive strategy to transform feminism—a strategy employed from the mid-seventies to the present. The attack on feminist racism in women's studies intensified as the academic field of women's studies was being institutionalized in the early eighties. I discuss the 1981 National Women's Studies Association conference, "Women Respond to

Racism." In this chapter, I argue that feminism is presently conceived as a movement which represents, in an uncomplicated form, the 'subjects' in politics. These subjects are seen to determine the character of feminism as well as its self-definition. Through attention to questions of organization, I shift the focus of debate from the subjects of feminism to the mechanisms and processes which produce feminism and its collective subject. As a methodological tool, organization allows one to envision feminism as a dialectical construct, not a mirror of the subject.

Organization, as an analytic category which mediates theory and practice, also takes into account the collective subject of 'political organization', or groups in politics. This collective subject derails the subject-based and largely individualist focus on a movement's or group's representation of its members. The collective subject of political solidarity does not attempt to embody the necessarily disparate collection of representative voices or positions within political movements. Neither does this collective subject analytically smooth over differences between politically identified subjects and formal organization. Importantly, the collective subject, when organization frames the inquiry, does not center on issues of subjectivity or the political identification of its members. Instead, organization highlights how specific political organizations produce their collective subject of social transformation.[20] This collective subject of organization demands we question the very mechanisms of representation, how a group or movement or collective proposes to "hear" the diverse opinions and positions and interests within its membership.[21] In this chapter, I begin to outline the relationship of struggle to this aspect of organization, since the category of struggle encompasses how decisions and policies are formulated within a collective entity, and how a group addresses structural socioeconomic divisions in that collective.

Chapter 3 explores the celebration of dissent in antiorganizational strategies to fight repression within feminism. As debates in the second wave women's movement richly illustrate, a women's movement committed to anti-elitism must reformulate accepted modes of representation and the relationship of a women's movement to other movements. These are both questions of leadership, since the ability of a movement to be open to the most oppressed and exploited women depends upon a movement that can also create its own conditions of possibility. As Jo Freeman (known as "Joreen") argues in her influential article "The Tyranny of Structurelessness", the outright rejection of structure cannot disavow entirely the informal methods of decision making or the structural relations that privilege who can make decisions.[22] Instead of trying to eradicate structure within the movement or group alone, an anti-elitist women's movement must create the organizational means to dismantle dominant hierarchies based on class, nationality, or race privilege.

In chapter 3, I demonstrate that even when antiorganizational feminists in the early women's liberation movement answered the question, Who leads? with, No one, another question arose: What leads? The shape of a movement, whatever its commitments, requires some degree of conscious organization and conscious struggle. Struggle unhinges even a contingent category feminism, or a fragmentary definition of women's movement as such. For example, Donna Haraway's cyborg illustrates the impossibility of a feminist movement that is stable or nonporous.[23] The cyborg contests any restrictive boundaries between feminism and other liberatory traditions. These boundaries, it convincingly demonstrates, could never simply exist in the first place. Haraway's emphasis on struggle highlights not feminism alone, but the wide range of potentially politicized subject formations. Her conclusions about feminism suggest its eventual irrelevance due to the liberating possibilities of technology, with more flexible coalitions and alliances—between subject positions, rather than between groups—to replace staid or outdated forms of formal political organization. In light of this view, I argue that antiorganizational feminist positions from the early seventies to the present reflect distrust of political organization itself, rather than distrust of the specific character of a political group or formation. Generally, their distrust of organization produces politics with an anarchist bent. But for Haraway, politics reside in the discursive formation of the subject rather than in any politics of (dis)unity.[24] Her focus on the construction of subject and the potential for rebellion within those relations atomizes politics beyond a distrust of authority or hierarchy. This individualism, collective only through common relations of power/production, creates politics with more of a libertarian (rather than anarchic) character.[25] In second wave theories about feminist struggle and women's political organization, feminism itself is not similarly delegitimized, but understood as a partial sphere of women's organization. These earlier theories of feminist struggles include theorizations of the organization of woman in civic, labor, and identity-conditional forms. Whereas present antiorganizational theories stress mutually relevant struggles through the subjects in politics, the second wave primarily explored the links between groups and movements.

In chapters 4 and 5, I build on those early feminist theories of women's organization that presume neither its collective subject woman, nor the formalization of a gendered solidarity into a women's movement. Three central issues regarding feminist struggle emerge from these early discussions about organization: the relationship of the women's movement (and feminism) to other progressive movements, methods of collective representation, and leadership. Chapter 4 shows how the issue of lesbian sexuality, whether figured as the fight against homophobia within the women's movement or as a larger critique against the nuclear family and enforced heterosexuality, demanded flexibility and permeability in cross-movement conceptions of political organization. As issues traverse movement boundaries, so too, struggle defies discrete theories of hermetically sealed political organization. Purist definitions of who a movement can (or should) represent, and rigid formulations of a movement's ideological boundaries give way or internally collapse in the face of energizing crosscurrents of activists, ideas, and issues. Struggle, discussed in chapter 4 through the issue of lesbian sexuality, revitalizes even as it challenges political organization—*because* it demands flexibility and innovation.

Feminist scholars continue to debate questions of movement interrelationship, representation, and leadership, though in less explicit terms. The early second wave analyses suggest that not only do theories of organizing women exceed the women's movement, but women's activism exceeds feminism. Disparate and partial, feminist acts of struggle inform and shape the women's movement, and not solely the other way around. In this sense, feminism is contingent not only due to contestation around subject formation, but also due to the demands of struggle. Paradoxically, the limit of struggle is also its realm of possibility. As unorganized and nonformal modes of struggle are formalized in organization, these creative impulses are given greater voice, even as its ephemeral passion may be muted.

Early writings about the second wave women's movement envision the organization of women and the women's movement in relation to other movements for transformative social change. The contradictory positions pitting a coherent or fully autonomous women's movement against a relational, semi-autonomous women's movement evince the fervent debate about intersections between movements. These contentions about the relationship of the women's movement to antiwar, Black Power, or student movements do not simply reveal the insecurities of a new movement, as many historians and analysts of the time would have it.[26] Instead, they flesh out how the ebullience (and indiscipline) of struggle can enrich formal political organization. Perhaps more surprisingly in our present era, which celebrates resistance but not insurrection, these debates illustrate the necessity of organization to manifest the liberatory possibilities of struggle. Political unity, as the organizational transformation of solidarity, is a prerequisite, and not merely the necessary evil, of revolutionary struggle.

In her much-cited interview with Gayatri Spivak, Ellen Rooney opens with a comment about feminist organizations and the ontological category 'woman'. She writes, "We seem to desire that what unites us [as feminists] pre-exist our desire to be joined."[27] Rooney discusses woman as the category operates within the collective entity feminism. In relation to struggle and organization, there are two parts to her observation. First, she describes the tendency to naturalize the political organization of women rather than show how women's political organization was produced. Second, she locates a presumption about an essentialist collective subject woman, one immanent in a similarly predestined process of struggle. She succinctly pinpoints the nondialectical constructions of feminism.

Rooney describes one tendency within feminism that attempts to resist the contingency of struggle: grounding the fleeting aspect of politics through an ontological basis for unity, whether through a naturalized collective subject woman or the political collectivity itself. Political unity, which Rooney figures through desire, is neither inevitable nor individualist, but a compulsion of political organization. Rather than read in "desire" a timeless dilemma of political foundations, I stress in her observation a subtle shift in focus from the idiosyncrasies of feminists to the organizational entity, feminism. In this sense, Rooney refers to a theory of feminist politics that preconceives neither theory nor practice in feminism. Instead, she suggests an organizational imagination that constructs the terms of its inquiry through political engagement. As a theory always in relation to politics, this organizational imagination is bounded by the vicissitudes of struggle.

The larger understanding of organization that informs a problematic category woman cannot be reached through theoretical tinkering with the concept of a movement's collective subject alone. Instead, the contingency of struggle must be viewed in relation to organization. Feminism as an organizational category can never fully be uniform or even consistent, since there is no visible formation 'women's movement' or way of seeing 'feminism'. Instead, these concepts preconceive political solidarity where there might be none. As I discuss in chapters 1 and 2, all women are not necessarily part of a women's movement simply because the name suggests a universal site for women's political solidarity. The essentialism of women's movement is a fallacy of its own making, since there is no unity to begin with, just a leap of faith that a gendered solidarity will materialize into a movement and that a movement can transform exploitative and oppressive relations of gender into something better. Organization is grounded, if in anything, in this political leap of faith. Lukacs describes joining the communist party as a similar kind of leap, as "the first *conscious* step towards the realm of freedom" (emphasis in original).[28] As a leap of faith, any invocation of feminism must presume some political coherence or unity. This invocation, however, is not a simple effect of political will or a voluntarist description of incremental and daily resistance. Even this act of faith, the invocation of political organization, includes the process of building solidarity, building unity, or building opposition.

Ann Snitow, in "Pages from a Gender Diary," also offers insight into the study of feminism, as she points toward the instability of organization as a methodological vantage point.[29] Snitow outlines a primary fault line in feminism, between a constructed (and therefore deconstructable) category 'woman' and its ontological inverse, an essential (and therefore unifying) 'woman'. She writes, "[A] common divide keeps forming in both feminist thought and action between the need to build the identity 'woman' and give it solid political meaning and the need to tear down the very category 'woman' and dismantle its all-too-solid history."[30] Rather than deplore the hypocrisy of feminist theoretical vagaries, Snitow sets this tension in its political context, as a necessarily shifting response to organizing women. Snitow frees ongoing debates around woman and feminism from charges of inconsistency or lack of theoretical rigor. Instead, she centers her analysis on the sites which demand different theories of woman in feminist politics. Snitow does not attempt to resolve theoretical differences or take sides on the opposition between woman as essence and woman as construction. In other words, she eschews the grander question of What is? to ask about a specifically political construct of the world. She isolates a self-conscious and oppositional political moment in the debate about woman to understand what theories of feminist opposition motivated and were motivated by coexisting yet irresolvable definitions of its collective subject woman.

The contingency of feminism lies in struggle, but the formalization—or making conscious—in Lukács' words, of these actions creates and reproduces political organization. That is, the accrual of struggle, historically and politically, is embedded within organization. And, as Rosa Luxemburg stresses in her definition of struggle, the formalization of goals and the analysis of political economy, vital aspects of organization, also shape struggle.[31] As a dialectical relationship, struggle cannot operate wholly autonomously from organization. In this sense, Luxemburg describes not only political organization, or movements and groups, but also organization as a methodological problem. To conceive of struggle outside of organization creates an idealist political analysis. To understand organization without recognition of struggle produces a determinist political analysis. Struggle in relation to organization demands a profoundly materialist analysis, both of the conditions determining revolutionary political agitation and the means to transform the historical bases of injustice and inequality. This book does not attempt to foreclose the discussion of what organization or struggle should produce politically. My goal is to join another kind of discussion about feminism, a discussion that overtly mediates practice and theory.

ONE

CONTINGENCY PLANS FOR THE
FEMINIST REVOLUTION

A 1998 cover of *Time* magazine broadcasts its apocalyptic question: "Is Feminism Dead?"[1] The *Time* story bolsters its predictions about the death of feminism by citing the declining numbers of women, particularly young women, who identify themselves as feminists.[2] The article inside caricatures the movement that its cover kills off by query. "Feminism: It's All About Me!" the title declares. The drift of this second title is also commonplace: nobody does politics anymore, and this cultural stuff going on with young people is at best lifestyle politics. Young people care more about transforming the individual body than the social polity. Young women, and youth more generally, have embraced the defensive posture of consumption politics: what they eat, what they wear, and what they buy. This potent mix—combining predictions of the movement's imminent death with a political irrelevance dominates media discussions of feminism and youth politics.[3]

Recent publications about third wave feminism are mostly collections of articles.[4] As at the inception of the women's liberation movement, the diversity of positions and ideas fueling interest in the third wave of feminism is accommodated anthology-style. Positions expressed in the collection, then as now, are contradictory and widely disparate in their concerns and ideas.[5] The writings about as yet diffuse politics suggest rather than state the contours of their subject. The most striking difference from earlier collections edited by Leslie Tanner, Toni Cade, Sookie Stambler, Edith Hoshino Altbach, and other better known feminists is that essays about third wave feminism are written, almost exclusively, in the first person.[6] The personal voice does not mean these articles are entirely about the writers. More general concerns emerge from many, though certainly not all, of these articles.

Anthologies of third wave feminism contain a related preoccupation: they present feminism as an identity they cannot fully embrace.[7] But these collections take their concerns a step further than *Time* analysts; they begin to reject feminism as an identity and wonder about feminism as a movement. In her introduction to one anthology about young people and feminism, entitled *To Be Real,* Rebecca Walker outlines this transition from feminism as an identity to feminism as a movement. Walker writes:

> For many of us it seems that to be a feminist in the way that we have seen or un-derstood feminism is to conform to an identity. . . . [T]ragically, rather than struggling to locate themselves within some continuum of feminism . . . many young women and men simply bow out altogether, avoiding the dreaded con-frontation with some of the people who presently define and represent feminism, and with their own beliefs.[8]

Walker rejects the simplistic characterization by conservative feminists of feminism as a dead or irrelevant movement, such as Christine Sommers' scathing assessment in her book *The Morning After*. Instead, Walker reframes the term feminism as a continuum rather than an identity. Feminism, then, is not solely a failed movement, though many of the critiques in Walker's volume presume a basic failure in second wave feminism. Feminism is a process. These articles suggest a third path: if young feminists disagree with current trends in feminism, their role must be to change rather than merely reject the movement. Third wave feminist articles, I suggest, are shifting away from feminism as an identity-defining movement towards a flexible, responsive movement, one that participants shape as the movement transforms them. Third wave feminists, in this respect, mirror early second wave activists of the women's liberation movement.

At this time of emerging possibilities for feminist movements, this chapter rein-troduces for collective discussion, or memory-work, that formative second wave par-adigm: reform-versus-revolution. The women's liberation movement (WLM) was predicted before it had a name, named before it was a movement, and imagined as revolutionary even when its politics were strictly reformist. This chapter theorizes the lessons of contingency from a movement forgotten long before its legacy dis-sipates. Present discussions about contingency in feminism center on the subject in politics and the tactics that develop in relation to that subject's conditions. We forget about the emergence and maintenance of revolutionary feminism when we focus so determinedly on questions of identity and subjectivity divorced from or-ganization. Professionally published essays by Margaret Benston and Juliet Mitchell, and early manifestoes, memos, and position papers, debated reform-versus-revolution in the tactics, forms, and strategies of the WLM to develop an understanding of how collective movements demand an enduring contingency. Most importantly for this period of an aspiring third wave of feminism, these de-bates remind us of an earlier center for feminist theories of social change: the po-litical movement.

This unearthed paradigm carries demands of its own. Early questions about how to build a revolutionary movement cannot be grafted onto our the-ories about the subject. A movement is composed of subjects and subjectivities, identities and consciousness, but it is not the sum of its parts. To a large degree, we have lost the tools to understand a movement as an entity. I draw on a debate over organization from the early twentieth century between Georg Lukács, Rosa Luxemburg, and V. I. Lenin to analyze the movement as a form of collective politics.[9] To attend to the concerns of organization is to envisage what feminism might configure now, and again in a past as rife with possibility as the present. As an ongoing process of contestation and configuration, emboldened demands, and inspired destruction, feminism must be seen as a movement located in its own organizational imagination as much as in a determinate period or social context.

The tension between reform and revolution predicated (even as it predicted) the women's liberation movement by debating how to build a revolutionary (rather than reformist) movement. Present time lines of the second wave women's movement discuss the movement as a series of debates between equality and difference. But early second wave analyses of political economy and their predictions about a revolutionary women's movement palpably illustrate a more movement-based site of departure. Debates about equality and difference are debates about subjects *in politics*. Early debates over reform and revolution, as they mapped the terrain through a study of political economy, ask about the movement and its social context as a whole. But two concerns regarding the political subject developed from these debates. The first is still voiced in present feminist debates: the subject in politics. The second concern—the subject *produced by* the political movement—has largely disappeared. This chapter takes a closer look at what present histories have occluded: the movement as a theoretical starting point to reevaluate an early second wave feminist methodology for an emerging movement.

In early writings about the women's movement an understanding of political economy illuminates how women are integrally linked to complex social, political, and economic relations of capitalism.[10] These writings draw out the connections between a revolutionary women's movement and the class struggle as well as struggles against racism.[11] In addition, the recognition of the political economy of women denies the immutability of these relations by revealing contradictions around gender and sex. As Margaret Benston's early essay argues even in its title, "The Political Economy of Women's Liberation," women's liberation is part of the purview of political economy.[12] But an analysis of political economy alone could not answer how to turn this understanding of social conditions into a revolutionary feminist platform or how to theorize the relation between reformist political work and revolutionary aims. To understand how to give political form to a systemic analysis of gender and to a women's liberation movement, we need to add other categories to our study: organization and struggle.

Georg Lukács defines organization as the intersection of theory and practice. In this sense, organization is a conceptual scope of analysis.[13] Women are not a natural constituency for politics, but the development of women as a political constituency takes particular paths that we can trace through myriad movements and groups. Organization guides subjects in politics to articulate what those paths are and where they lead. Mitchell and Benston, through their analyses of the political economy of women, suggest very different possibilities for the women's liberation movement. Mitchell's analysis endorses the traditional left prerequisite for a revolutionary feminism: shift women from unpaid reproductive labor to paid productive work. Benston includes another important precondition: transform the relations of reproductive labor from atomized and unpaid into communal and commodified. As an impetus for future campaigns, demands, and strategies, Benston's article adds another site for revolutionary feminist politics: domestic labor.

Embedded in the larger socioeconomic context of the movement are pointedly strategic questions. How do we build a strong group/movement? Whom do we want to approach? How do we frame our issues? These questions all pertain to the methods of political activism. Additional questions are: Who are our subjects? What are our objects? How do these subject/objects meet in politics? Most studies of particular groups or social movements relay information about organization, even if the junctures between theory and practice are not explicitly outlined and even if the concept of organization is not theorized. Mitchell suggests the workplace as a primary site for a revolutionary feminist movement. Benston casts a much wider net, potentially including the home, the shopping center, the park, and other places where women congregate as domestic laborers. What defines women in a women's liberation movement in these two visions, correspondingly, will differ widely. Through their different conclusions about the political economy of women, Mitchell and Benston generate different sites, subjects, and methods for revolutionary feminism.

Organization as a category of analysis does not just illuminate the political methods employed, but helps to raise a more speculative question: Where will it end? What do we want to achieve? How can we go from here to there? And, at the center of this book, the question: what *can* these politics produce? More specifically, what are the limits of the different constructions of gender and women in politics? Both sets of questions, whether about political tools or political goals, demand that the intersection of theory and practice produce full answers. Mitchell and Benston share a common goal, the liberation of women. Both look beyond the formal equality between women and men toward transforming the social and political relations that bind women and men. But Mitchell harnesses changes in reproductive labor to those in productive labor, linking changes in unpaid "women's work" to struggles in the paid workplace. Benston creates two additional trajectories for a revolutionary feminism: first, toward a reversal of this causality, second, toward a political semi-autonomy between the two sites.

A more comprehensive study must also look at centrist and right-wing theories of organizing women, since the concept of organization does not delimit the field of questioning to leftist politics. However, for a leftist or revolutionary movement, organization has particular implications, even in a scholarly study of organization. To ask what is organization, then, is not the same question for leftist, liberal, or conservative politics, since the character of politics and the demands of those politics on organization transform the object of study.

TIME LINES AND SECOND WAVE
RECONSTRUCTIONS

Recent books about the second wave women's movement stress the movement's contradictory, contestatory, and noncontiguous character through revealing detail. Daniel Horowitz's biography of Betty Friedan extends our knowledge of feminism's many debts, not just to other movements like the communist Left, civil rights, and peace movements, but more surprisingly to the Cold War.[14] Horowitz builds on an often implicit thesis about the constitutive influence of conservatism on feminism in books about women's politics in the late forties to early sixties, such as Leila Rupp and Verta Taylor's groundbreaking history, *Survival in the Doldrums: The American Women's Rights Movement, 1945 to the 1960s*.[15] He underscores how the conservative forces of anticommunism shaped Friedan's choice of middle-class housewives as the audience and subject for *The Feminine Mystique*. Horowitz shows how the goal of women's equality was deeply embedded in McCarthyist political repression as it scaled back more radical, and more threatening demands for women's freedom or women's liberation.

Elizabeth Guy-Shefthall's anthology, entitled *Words of Fire: An Anthology of African-American Feminist Thought*, reintroduces the confrontations of feminist ideas with Cold War politics (and the usurpation of those ideas by the latter) though the writings of Lorraine Hansberry, Claudia Jones, and Florynce Kennedy. Guy-Shefthall's volume also celebrates the ephemeral quality of much early second wave feminist writing. She draws together essays often passed around as photostats of hand-written documents, like "A Historical and Critical Essay for Black Women" by Patricia Haden, Donna Middleton, and Patricia Robinson, and essays that served as manifestoes for new formations, such as Mary Ann Weathers's "An Argument for Black Women's Liberation as a Revolutionary Force." Guy-Shefthall combines essays whose authors do not share the same political affiliations—even take oppositional positions—and establishes an internally contradictory canon of African-American feminist thought. By retaining these ideological contradictions, Guy-Shefthall's volume undermines essentialist definitions of a single African-American feminist constituency and history.[16]

Such anthologies as Guy-Shefthall's, Alma Garcia's *(Chicana Feminist Thought: The Basic Historical Writings)*, and Barbara Crow's *(Radical Feminism: A Documentary Reader)* embrace the lack of a consensus, the sheer messiness of feminism, as they showcase the wide diversity of Chicano, African-American, and radical feminist thought. These writings shaped (as often as they were ignored) constructions of the radical and youth-oriented women's liberation movement. This respect for the ephemera generated in the women's movement, and for its importance to our understanding of feminism, also animates Katie King's wide-ranging book, *Theory in Its Feminist Travels: Conversations in U.S. Women's Movements*.[17] She figures her conversations not as distinct voices with coherent arguments, but as overlapping positions and dynamic illustrations of the lack of proximity between feminisms.[18] Because King refuses to stabilize her objects of study, she cannily reveals power relations within the women's movement as histories and memories continue to construct it. She writes about black women's marginalization from the women's movement and the methodological implications of this marginalization:

> But I think this formulation/assumption of white women at the center masks the other possibility, the one implied by Stimpson's "envious" description of the Black movement, another evaluation that white women are newcomers, not at all at a preexisting center on the outskirts of the Black movement and other social justice movements, and of the new left. . . . White privilege and radical white women's difficult experiences in the new left combine with Echols's formulation of radical feminism's claims of autonomy to produce a shifting illusion/reality newly/retrospectively centering white women, in the political imagination of white women's liberations, as "the feminist struggle."[19]

King suggests how the singularity of feminism masks internal debates and power struggles to define feminism. She illustrates the productive incoherence of even a movement as such. She, like Guy-Shefthall, Crow, and Garcia, shows feminist plurality not as a recent and enlightened corrective to past mistakes, a simple game of numbers and recognition, but as a question of research, methodology, and ideology.

Other anthologies nod to the richness of feminist ephemera as theory. Rosemary Hennessey and Chrys Ingraham's collection, *Materialist Feminism,* consolidates its theoretical object, materialist feminism, as a second wave concern through its inclusion of work by Margaret Benston, Mary Alice Waters, and Selma James.[20] But this respect for largely unknown writers and nonprofessional writings does not define the field. In *The Second Wave: A Reader in Feminist Theory,* Linda Nicholson purports to assemble the central texts of the women's movement we call the second wave.[21] However, she includes only two ephemeral texts in her selection (also the only ones to voice concern about revolutionary change), Radicalesbians' "The Woman-Identified Woman," first distributed in 1970, and the Combahee River Collective's "A Black Feminist Statement." Nicholson's volume also skips every professionally published essay between 1964 and 1974 with the exception of a brief excerpt from Shulamith Firestone's *The Dialectic of Sex.* Reemerging with Gayle Rubin's "The Traffic in Women," Nicholson effectively mutes formative debates about how to define women's movement and enact feminism.

Nancy Fraser's most recent book, *Justice Interruptus,* has a related theoretical amnesia, one that might explain the chronological and ideological gap in Nicholson's volume. Fraser relies on the analytic paradigm of equality-versus-difference to constitute feminist theory as a body of knowledge and politics.[22] Fraser's essay in the book, "Multiculturalism, Antiessentialism, and Radical Democracy," reassesses the philosophical boundaries of contemporary debates about social, political, and economic justice and finds them wanting. The recognition of differences, she contends, has overtaken concerns about the redistribution of resources. To counteract this disturbing trend, Fraser persuasively argues that feminist analyses must once again address issues of political economy. An analysis of political economy would provide a more complex, critical, and long-term view of social transformation, one that can revitalize these neglected facets of feminism. She outlines the theoretical legacy of American second wave feminism from the sixties onward and draws upon its animated debates over equality and difference to support her proposal.

Fraser characterizes the questions of second wave feminism through a thematic time line. In the early stages of the second wave women's movement, feminism debated equality-versus-difference; from the mid-eighties, differences between women; and since the early nineties, multiple and intersecting differences. Fraser sets up a misleadingly causal relationship between early debates about women's equality with the intellectual inquiries that followed. These reformulations in feminism regarding differences between women and intersecting differences among women, Fraser argues, undermined the dominance of equality as a political goal. Equality, in Fraser's description, presumes that women's status should be commensurate to men's. As a conceptual focus, equality aims to end gender difference (as *the* basis for discrimination against women) altogether.[23] Fraser describes how equality, as feminism's political and analytic lens, discredited another strategy: revaluing gender differences, both cultural and biological.[24]

To lump the first ten-plus years of second wave feminism, from the mid-sixties to the late seventies, into the rubric of equality-versus-difference (a formulation first articulated in the early eighties) is to truncate severely the political memory of the women's movement.[25] Unfortunately, due to the influential (and often brilliant) essay by Ann Snitow, "Pages from a Gender Diary," about early radical feminism, and the history by Alice Echols, *Daring to be Bad,* among other recent accounts, feminist scholars have collapsed rich debates about equality, liberation, and freedom into a dichotomy between equality and difference.[26]

As a means to order disparate positions, writings, and campaigns, 'difference' provides an attractive framework, since it can refer to contestation over dichotomized biological difference, essentialist differences between women and men, and political separatism. Both Snitow and Echols write about a vocal fragment of the women's movement, a fragment, even, of the more general denomination "women's liberation movement." They discuss a feminism often called "radical" at the time, growing out of the youth movement on campuses and in the South. Although neither Snitow nor Echols claims to write about the whole of the early women's movement, radical feminism increasingly stands in for that wide spectrum of politics. Perhaps equality-versus-difference explains a central debate within radical feminism, but this characterization is too limited for the range of questions faced by the women's movement as a whole. The women's liberation movement, understood as those groups identified by name, and more generously conceived as a noncontiguous set of political formations, rises from another question, about what kind of movement to build. Reform-versus-revolution, as a question of possibility and invention, characterizes the stakes of early second wave feminist debates with much greater accuracy than does equality-versus-difference.[27]

Fraser's truncation of second wave feminism and Nicholson's forgotten period encompass some of the largest political fights launched by feminists, over the Equal Rights Amendment and comparable worth, and struggles within feminism over structural racism, lesbians, and sexuality in the movement. Theoretically, this erasure of goals, ideas, and battles is more disturbing. This formative period in the late sixties to the mid seventies, with its widely disparate and unstable definitions of feminism, was a socioeconomically, racially, and substantively diverse (and contentious) period of feminist politics. From the early sixties to the early seventies, feminist writings grapple most directly with questions of conscious organization and the dialectical relationship between theory and practice. We lose, in effect, the chance to take the women's movement into account on its own terms.

As an analytic framework, equality-versus-difference can illuminate how the subjects of feminism position the women's movement through its vision of itself and the goals, strategies, and tactics it endorses.[28] Equality-versus-difference can explain movement separatism as an outgrowth of feminist analysis of the political economy of patriarchy. Equality-versus-difference admits the complex interconnections between theory and practice, but it forecloses the early women's movement as both subject and object of its construction. Revolution-versus-reform didn't encompass all early debates about the possibility of feminism or the women's liberation movement, but it can suggest formulations feminism still abides by, theories the women's movement still constructs itself around. Most importantly, reform-versus-revolution lays the groundwork for a valuable conceptual assumption in early second wave thought, one rare in discussions about feminism today: that of political organization and feminism.[29]

Disparate views on the political economy of women and women's liberation fueled the debate over how to build revolutionary rather than reformist politics. This argument raged throughout the mid-sixties to the seventies and spanned Leftist political movements and campaigns.[30] With the exception of Fraser's resuscitation of political economy, these once fiery positions and counterpositions in the women's movement have left very few theoretical traces in the writings of academic feminism.[31] Feminism of the late nineties has not renounced its historical beginnings in impassioned speeches, innovative campaigns, and combative guerilla theater, but we have lost much of their content. The force of recent analyses and their targets of critique have been remembered in abbreviated ways that simplify their goals and strategies. Most glaringly, we have forgotten the subject of these debates: the collective movement itself.

Insights generated by understanding political economy enabled early projections of the women's liberation movement and lent definition to ongoing movements and their socio-political contexts. These insights helped theorists and activities to envision that movement's urealized possibilities and to elaborate its strategies and long-term goals. When we ask about the WLM and its conditions of possibility, debates over reform-versus-revolution center on the movement's form, method, analysis, and structure. From a question about the unstable and embattled subject in politics we must ask about the production of an entire range of political processes. A study of organization, in Lukács's terms, "makes conscious" the movement's theoretical assumptions about its politics.

ORGANIZATION AND STRUGGLE

Early debates about the political economy of women and women's liberation opened rich discussions about feminism as the basis for a revolutionary movement. But an understanding of political economy alone does not shed light on how to enact the possibilities uncovered. We have reached a theoretical impasse, without terms to discuss the present forms of politics, the tools of political engagement, or where these formations might lead.

In political theory, the clearest discussion of how to enact and imagine politics is in debates between Lukács, Lenin, and Luxemburg from the 1900s through the 1920s.[32] While they debate problems of the constitution of a vanguard, proletarian, democratic-centralist communist party, nonetheless their discussions raise questions of organizational form more generally. For our purposes, the categories of organization and struggle are of the most use. Organization prefigures that political possibility, a women's movement, and suggests how women as a political category generates its own possibilities for a movement in three ways: as a scope of study, an analytic category, and a methodology. As a scope of study, organization blurs distinctions between theory and practice, but not through the deconstruction of this dichotomy. Instead, as the site where theory meets practice, organization attempts to understand their dialectical interdependency.

Analytically, organization allows us to examine what theories that animated early WLM politics, and gives us the means to trace how early second wave feminist ideologies about revolutionary politics both enabled and limited decisions made by feminist activists. In this discussion, I trace two analytic concerns to help refigure feminism and women's liberation movement as collective bodies. The first, representation, raises questions about the accountability of the movement to its own theories of social transformation. As theory must be accountable to—that is, represent—the ideals and goals of a movement, so too the movement must work to answer its own ideological demands. The second, leadership, is related since it asks, What determines feminism, theory or practice? Questions of organization and leadership help to elaborate that much-commented-on quality of feminism: its diffuseness, its lack of discrete boundaries, and its conscious embrace of the contingent and sometimes momentary political object-status.

As a methodology, organization sheds light on causal relations between a movement and its social context. The political imaginary is a realm of theoretical ideals that limits and enables a movement as much as its material conditions do. In the case of the WLM, the commitment to women meant that revolutionary affiliations were bound to incremental reformist struggles, like the fight for child care.[33] In addition, even when the WLM theorized itself as a separate movement, it could not divorce itself entirely from the larger arena of political struggles and retain its revolutionary (as opposed to reformist) ideals.[34] Also, methodologically, an organizational analysis severely curtails the predominance of subject-centered political agency. A study of organization suggests how the women's liberation movement produces its subjects of politics even as those subjects create and sustain the movement. Women, even as activists or supporters of the WLM, are as much a construction of the movement's theories and politics as any material conditions that construct women as a social grouping.

Lukács, in his essay "Towards a Methodology of the Problem of Organization," defines organization as a "dialectical category."[35] "Organization is the form of mediation between theory and practice. And, as in every dialectical relationship, the terms of the relation only acquire concreteness and reality in and by virtue of this mediation."[36] Lukács uses the two terms "form" and "relation" simultaneously to describe it. As a form of mediation, organization refers to an object; but as a relation, organization refers to active processes. Both aspects constitute the colloquial inferences of organization; first, that it is a thing, and second, that it is something one does (Lukács calls both aspects the "technical parts" of organization). Yet organization exceeds both of these colloquial senses as the site for a dialectical relationship where theory and practice interact. Theory and practice are not situated in opposition to each other, nor hierarchically in relation to each other, but are interdependent *in the form of organization*. Organization is always about political construction: its forms and theories.

Organization here does not merely refer to the specific groups in a larger movement, nor does it refer to the various processes of agitation. That is, organization does not provide the means to catalogue the collectivities that are part of a political landscape. So, the National Organization of Women (NOW) is not an example of organization's mediation between, say, academics and activists, but one example of a political organization among many. Nor is organization a coded reference to organizing, or a pure act of doing politics (often in opposition to just thinking about politics, as in the case of the much-reviled "armchair Marxists"). Organization is neither as substantively thing-like as a political group, nor as spontaneous and diffuse as acting out one's beliefs. Organization, in the Marxist tradition, has a richer meaning than either description can account for.

Both colloquial definitions of organization operate as simple referents, seemingly transparent actions or things that dismiss the possibility (or need) of theorizing them. Part of their transparency has to do with the self-evidence of the qualities that define them: whether it be a group's charter document or the motions of handing out leaflets. In addition, organization in both senses reinforces a reified definition of politics against a necessarily idealist theory, even though both the distribution of leaflets and the production of a charter document involve theoretical labor. To join (or, better yet, to form) an avowedly political group is to enact one's ideological affiliations just as much as agitating for changes in working conditions. Both colloquial senses of organization, at the outset, embody politics. In this manner, they reinforce rather than mediate the split between theory and politics.

One place to begin a counterdefinition is the title of Lenin's volume of essays that debate ongoing questions of revolutionary versus reformist organization in

Marxism: *What Is to Be Done?*[37] Organization, in Lenin's writings, is not just the empirical details and accruals of politics. Instead, organization is a variegated field, a site of many parts, wherein theory and politics have mutually dependent roles. Three basic parts of organization emerge from Lenin's work, illustrated by his book's title. The title contains a theoretical imperative within a question of constructive tasks. Lenin asks a question about organizing, What must revolutionaries do? However, the verb *to be* forestalls the actual processes of doing to ask not only what next, but *why choose* that course of action. In Lenin's account, viable organizing needs a long-term vision, and participants must ask not only what should be done today, but what should be done for tomorrow—given the conditions of the political economy. Organizational questions cannot end at what is possible in the present conditions, but must project how a revolutionary movement can shape the conditions of the future.[38] As an interrogative, *What is to be Done?* demands an analysis of the present situation, a theory about what to strive for, and a plan describing how to build from present conditions toward future goals. Organization encompasses all three of these projects.

Two theoretical issues emerge from this definition of organization: representation and leadership. On the question of representation, the debate centers on the group or movement as the *collective representation* of politics and of its members. But the movement/group is as responsible for its promises, goals, and strategies as it is for the carrying out of its members' will or interests. The women's movement did not arise solely from a few charismatic or far-seeing people, nor from a wellspring of support by a mass constituency. The women's movement gained form from its self-definition, through its campaigns, goals, and ideals. Organization as an analytic focus produces greater accountability of a movement to its members and leaders, since it reveals how a movement or group constructs itself, its forms, ideals, and program. A revolutionary understanding of political organization transcends populist-democratic theories of representation, which simply demand the accountability of leaders to members (or the elimination of leader/members, the member-as-leader and vice versa). The question shifts from "who leads the movement" to "what leads the movement" and focuses on the movement's theoretical commitments over powerful leaders.[39]

Liberal models of political organization suggest two diametrically opposed alternatives: structure versus agency. The view of political organization as structure argues that the collective is paramount, and individuals are subordinate to the group as a monolithic entity; the view of political organization as agency proposes a model where the collective is the sum of autonomous individuals. This antimony dismisses the dialectic of individual/group, since individuals form and work in groups, but they are also produced by these relations. Therefore, a dialectical approach to the question of collective representation needs to be elaborated for political organization to mediate (rather than just enact or concretize) theory and practice.

Likewise, a movement must be accountable not simply to its membership or its leadership, but to its own visions and goals for social change. A result of organizational accountability: the movement is understood through its own terms. Rather than being an inert (and omnipotent) object or simple addition of forces and people, the collective movement has a logic and a dialectic of its own. Political subjects produce the movement, that is, they build the structures of governance and develop the terms of political engagement. But this movement produced by political subjects also projects its political subjects and subjectivities. This conception of political organization does not denigrate agency within political formations, nor the choices involved in political acts. It does, however, subvert causal, deterministic, or fatalistic explanations for any movement. This understanding of political organization diminishes control (assumed to reside in individuals and collections of individuals) over the movement. Political organization, as a collective formation, must carry the weight of its production and reproduction. An organizational analysis requires an abstract collectivity that is neither individualistic nor a sum of its parts, but one that represents that imagined whole, the movement. This alternate conception of a movement or group accounts for its effects through its theoretical production. In this sense, an analysis of organization suggests future possibilities and goals based on a political theory of what is to be done.[40] Thus, an analysis of organization makes visible the mechanisms of decision-making and representation at work, even those of a diffuse, ever-shifting movement.

Rosa Luxemburg introduces the regenerative possibilities for organization in spontaneous struggle. To understand the forms within the WLM in the United States, Luxemburg's careful delineation of struggle as part of, but also separate from, organization provides valuable insights. In *The Mass Strike, The Political Party and The Trade Unions*, first published in 1906, Rosa Luxemburg defines organization through its centrality to leadership, a leadership which can produce its own forms of struggle. But she also celebrates the untamed methods of struggle, forms that did not ground themselves in their relation to theory. Struggle, Luxemburg emphasizes, is not synonymous with, nor should it be wholly subsumed by, the site of organization. Organization produces consciousness about how decisions are derived and how the party or movement embodies the goals and insights it builds in practice/theory. Struggle, in relation to organization, may or may not manifest the goals and methods of revolutionary politics.

Luxemburg concentrates on how the vitality of struggle complicates any simple notion of political leadership and organization. In her support for an unorganized form of struggle, the mass strike, she argues that organization, or those movement politics accountable to its theories, must draw from its ingenuity. She writes, "[T]he apparently 'chaotic' strikes and the 'disorganized' revolutionary action after the January general strike is becoming the starting point of a feverish *work of organization*" (her emphasis).[41] Mass strikes themselves do not create revolution, nor do they produce revolutionary changes. Instead, they produce the conditions for the organizational work to begin, and can enable other forms of political leadership to arise. If analyzed in relation to organization, struggle can develop from unanticipated, spontaneous actions into conscious politics.

Luxemburg criticizes the Social Democratic Party (SDP)'s solely technical understanding of struggle. "The rigid, mechanical-bureaucratic conception cannot conceive of struggle save as the product of organization at a certain stage of its strength. On the contrary, the living, dialectical explanation makes the organization arise as a product of the struggle."[42] By positing a dialectical relationship between struggle and organization, Luxemburg argues for a wider category 'politics' to include myriad forms of opposition. Luxemburg's open-ended definition of politics allows even early, inchoate feminist formations to be included in an assessment of the women's liberation movement. The WLM began with unorganized struggle, but only became a movement through organization. Through a name and self-conception, the WLM gained its shape-shifting organizational form, only possible because the movement(s) never wholly rescinded the claims of unorganized struggle. Organization never fully led feminist struggle in the women's liberation movement.

REVOLUTIONARY PRECONDITIONS AND PREDICTIONS FOR SECOND WAVE FEMINISM

To pluck the phase *reform-versus-revolution* from the women's movement archives, in some respects, is arbitrary. The phrase functioned more like a slogan (though not one for posters or rallies) than a well-structured argument for particular feminist goals or politics. In fact, this term rarely shows up in professionally published essays about the women's liberation movement, but it captures the framework of written arguments about the women's liberation movement between 1965 and roughly 1973. While the term *revolution* remained after 1973, it no longer shaped itself in opposition to reform. This struggle between reform and revolution led to the conceptualization of a movement that favored the goal of liberation over equality. As a snippet from another time, reform-versus-revolution does not embody the whole story of early second wave feminism; instead, the phrase reveals a set of constructions and a political trajectory the women's movement left behind. To ignore ephemeral sources is to miss the primary records of the feminist theory for revolutionary politics, and I cite these sources often not for their prominence, but their clarity. This national struggle/debate was waged through position papers, letters, underground journals such as *Leviathan* and *Voice of the Women's Liberation Movement,* groups' publications such as *National SNCC Monthly* and *Revolutionary Age,* and movement presses such as New England Free Press and Radical Women Publications.

As early as 1970, Marlene Dixon in her essay "Where are We Going?" targets the nexus between theory and politics as the means to build a women's movement.[43] Dixon, an astute observer of the early women's movement, denounces the quality of feminist theory at the 1968 conference for radical feminists in Lake Villa, Illinois, attended by movement activists from the United States and Canada.[44] She wrote about debates that pitted advocates of consciousness-raising against adherents of such tactics as guerilla theater and demonstrations. Her critique does not target the often contentious character of the conference forums and papers, but focuses instead on the impoverished products of this dissent. She writes, "[T]he trouble was that none of these analyses, and this unfortunately especially applied to radical women, seriously linked theory and practice in such a way as to lead to strategies for action."[45] Dixon pinpoints the disjuncture between theory and practice as the reason for aimlessness in the burgeoning women's movement. While she does not call the confluence of theory and practice "organization," Dixon argues that by linking theory and practice, analyses can produce strategies for the women's movement in its acrimonious diversity. In her account of the 1968 conference, debates about the correct approach to the women's movement lacked the means even *to lead to* ideas of, in Dixon's words, "where to go."

The 1968 conference was part of a movement that set itself apart from the interest politics of reformist groups such as NOW. Women's liberation rejected the politics of women's rights as a bourgeois movement to alleviate the excesses of capitalism without changing an exploitative system. Yet, within the revolutionary ascriptions of women's liberation, organization as the nexus between theory and politics receded in the early to mid-seventies as a means to scrutinize feminist politics. Much of the movement in the mid-seventies took on a mystical quality, signifying women's necessary, if presently incomplete, unity. But this analytic and political decline of efforts to build a feminist movement cannot stand as the summary of the early second wave women's movement's legacy. As the reform-versus-revolution debate illustrates, the essentialism of women and a correspondingly essentialist movement in feminism was not inevitable, but a site of contestation. The women's movement, particularly its revolutionary strands, consistently questioned its own production of women and movement.

Juliet Mitchell wrote her enormously influential essay "Women: The Longest Revolution" before the women's liberation movement had even named itself. Effectively, Mitchell's essay announces the arrival of an organizational methodology for women's liberation before any such movement had congealed. She begins from the dialectical possibilities within 'women's conditions' that De Beauvoir so meticulously described in *The Second Sex*.[46] From De Beauvoir's detailed history of social relations around gender, Mitchell builds an analytic category, woman's conditions, to disrupt the timeless and inevitable qualities in the state of women. From women's conditions as an analytic category, Mitchell constructs an analysis of the political economy of women that can build a political movement. For Mitchell, an examination of women's conditions never remains at the level of what presently exists, but also probes what those conditions can produce. Mitchell asks how the conditions of women's oppression can create the transformation.

Mitchell's essay spares neither the party-based Left for its neglect of the woman question in its complexity, nor feminist theories for their lackadasical attitude toward socialist transformation. She positions her essay as one that addresses the task left incomplete by De Beauvoir's *The Second Sex*: the task of theorizing women through careful attention to organization.[47] Mitchell praises the scope and understanding of De Beauvoir's work, but she criticizes the "muffled" endorsement of socialism. She argues that De Beauvoir fails to give any indication of how socialism *could* produce any change: "[It] is not easy to see why socialism should modify the basic 'ontological' desire for a thing-like freedom which De Beauvoir sees as the motor behind the fixation with inheritance in the property system, or the enslavement of women which derived from it."[48] She attacks the ahistoricity attributed to women's conditions in De Beauvoir's analysis, and, more importantly, she decries the lack of any organizational dynamic to change these conditions. Instead, Mitchell approaches the question that remains unasked in a seemingly foreclosed evolution of women in history: What contradictions in woman's condition enable *opposition to* women's enslavement?

Mitchell draws from Althusser to redress unsubstantiated visions of women's emancipation within economist and ideological socialist analyses. She proposes the beginnings for an explicitly organizational theory of feminism:

> What is the solution to this impasse? It must lie in differentiating woman's condition, much more radically than in the past, into its separate structures, which together form a complex—not simple—unity. This will mean rejecting the idea that woman's condition can be deduced derivatively from the economy or equated symbolically with society. Rather it must be seen as a specific structure, which is a unity of different elements.[49]

Unlike her overview of De Beauvoir's argument, which refers to *women's* conditions, Mitchell uses the singular form *woman* to describe her own methodological prescription. Mitchell does not favor a closer or more accurate study into what women actually experience. Instead, as with the phrase *woman question* used in marxist writings, *woman's conditions* refers to socially produced relations as a dialectical field of inquiry and potential opposition. Woman's condition, in this sense, within its premise embeds the political transformation of that condition.

Mitchell does not predict the exact forms of the women's liberation movement in her essay, but she does prefigure women's liberation through her analysis of the political economy of women. Her radical rewriting of De Beauvoir can only imagine women as a political force through the dialectical relationship of woman's condition in the social totality. Mitchell's essay pushes a use of organization that analyses social totality to the fore of a liberatory analysis of woman. The political economy of woman's conditions, for Mitchell, suggests a social totality rife with contradictions, a totality unstable enough for a revolutionary transformation.

The women's movement, in Margaret Benston's "The Political Economy of Women's Liberation," is still largely a subtext, defined more by such (particular) struggles such as the fight against sexism in the New Left, day care for working women, and reproductive rights, than by an overarching ideological vision. Many of these debates center around pragmatic questions of building a revolutionary women's movement: how to relate to other revolutionary movements, whether to include all women's struggles, and how to draw more women into revolutionary politics.[50] Early theories that address the political economy of women and women's liberation do not answer the particular questions of the emerging movement. Instead, they ask more generally how reformist struggles can enrich a revolutionary political organization.

Benston wrote her article about women's liberation as a distinct movement even as the movement took shape in loosely connected groups around the country, but she was not the first to predict a revolutionary women's movement. Clara Fraser presented her explosive position paper about race and gender in social movements at the 1965 national convention of the Socialist Workers' Party (SWP). She subsequently published the section on the woman question under the generic title "The Emancipation of Women."[51] Her analysis of the woman question was one important ideological catalyst in the formation of the breakaway Freedom Socialist Party (FSP). Clara Fraser's paper lauds the civil rights movement for infusing social activism with revolutionary possibility. In addition, the paper does not just mention internal struggles for women's emancipation or its general character but predicts the formation of a radical women's movement out of the civil rights movement.

Fraser probably wrote (or at least edited) her essay after the distribution of Casey Hayden and Mary King's 1965 critique of sexism in the Student Non-Violent Coordinating Committee (SNCC), "A Kind of Memo."[52] Unlike Hayden and King, Clara Fraser does not solely attack sexism within gender-mixed organizations, neither does she imagine a unitary group's formation like NOW. She draws on her analysis of the political economy to produce her startling thesis: the revolutionary emancipation of women requires a separate movement. She credits civil rights struggles with providing "the training ground for the movement of women's emancipation, and each strengthens the other."[53] Fraser never delineates the scope of this women's movement; yet her prediction takes on an already embodied character through her use of the present tense: each movement already "*strengthens* the other"(emphasis added). In the blink of an eye, the civil rights and women's movements are not coterminous but separate movements. However, the preconditions for a radical women's movement lies with the production of activists in another struggle, one for black liberation. The movement for civil rights produces the preconditions for a radical women's movement. In Fraser's view these movements, though separate, are not in competition with each other, since she emphasizes the interdependency of their power. An analysis informed by political economy enabled the women's liberation movement. It allowed Mitchell, Benston, and Fraser to imagine such a movement was possible and necessary.

Not all theorists drew these conclusions from their analyses of the political economy of women or women's liberation. Joan Jordan, a member of the SWP, did not foresee a revolutionary movement for women, though after a women's movement arose she actively participated through the formation of such working women's groups as Mothers Alone Working and Women, Inc., in the Bay Area. Jordan projected an increase in women's bureaus to heighten working women's participation in unions, and a resulting pressure for the kinds of issues raised by those unions. She writes that it is "only in the last few decades that women's strategic position, her assimilation in industry, has so altered as to make [that] emancipation an urgent necessity."[54] Jordan's analysis predicts an increase in women's leadership and push for emancipation within the labor movement and economic production more generally, but not the rise of a distinct movement.

Unlike when Mitchell, Fraser, and Jordan published their writings discussed above, by the time Benston's essay was published in 1969, the term women's liberation had gained currency and described a movement. This movement had a name but still struggled to imagine its contours. The movement had gained revolutionary goals and a separate status from other movements, but not a clear sense of the politics and groups it represented. For this named movement, Benston proposes another beginning that reinforces its indeterminacy as a movement:

> We lack a corresponding structural definition of women. What is needed first is
> not a complete examination of the symptoms of the secondary status of women,
> but instead a statement of the material conditions in capitalist (and other) societies which define the group "women."[55]

She breaks Mitchell's category woman's conditions into its parts: 'women' and 'conditions'. Women retains its historicity and contradictory place within capitalism, but women have no natural interests defined through these conditions. Women is wholly produced even in the term's plural form. As Benston states bluntly, the elaboration of women's experience of secondary status cannot sustain women's liberation. Benston further destabilizes movement, since neither biological sex nor the lived experiences of women grounds its formation.

Benston's analysis of women's relationship to the means of production is not just an exercise in marxist theory, but a polemic designed to guide the women's liberation movement. This aspect of her analysis, this prescriptive element in relation to a political movement, makes her political economy, as the title proclaims, a political economy of women's liberation. Benston argues that women are defined by a relationship to the means of production that is different than men's. She writes:

> This assignment of household work as the function of a special category
> "women" means that this group *does* stand in a different relation to production
> than the group "men." We will tentatively define women, then, as that group of
> people which is responsible for the production of simple use-values in those activities associated with the home and family.[56]

Unlike Mitchell, who attempts to provide an overview of the complexity of women's conditions, Benston focuses on the aspect of women's definition in relation to production. She confronts what Mitchell calls "economism," arguing that by jumping so quickly to the superstructural aspects of women's conditions Mitchell misses the importance of the relations of production to the women's liberation movement. Unlike Mitchell's, Benston's analysis supports a contingent category, women, for a liberation movement.

When Benston extends Mitchell's argument about the need for women to join the paid workforce, she states that two preconditions for women's liberation are based on this definition of women. First, a movement for women's liberation must bring private production into public production. Second, this public production should not merely be made more efficient through communalization, but made part of the public economy. She argues that the transition is not just to support women's economic and political independence, but to transform the relations of reproduction. Moreover, women, she writes, are also waged workers, but their relationship to the private and unwaged work of reproduction defines women as a socioeconomic category. Thus, for Benston, waged work, transformed by these two conditions, would change women.

Benston's argument for a revolutionary but diffuse movement for contingently defined women ran counter to more essentialist arguments about the WLM. A narrative of women's oppression grounded in the origins of that oppression imparted an ethico-political strength to Shulamith Firestone's theory of a separate women's liberation movement that leads all movements.[57] Firestone writes, "[F]eminists have to question, not just all of *Western* culture, but the organization of culture itself, and further, even the very organization of nature."[58] As a more deeply embedded oppression, Firestone argues that a revolutionary feminism leads all movements through the strength of its comprehensive ideology. Less concerned with foundations than with the translation of women's oppression into political goals and campaigns, Benston does not set up a competition between class exploitation and gender-based oppression. Instead, she imagines women's liberation as a movement, but as one related to a wider movement for revolution. She ends her essay with an admonition to Left feminists: "[O]ur task is to make sure the revolutionary changes in the society do in fact end women's oppression."[59]

Benston celebrated an amorphous category 'movement' through her unstable category 'women'. But her detailed plan of action also attempts to envision what revolution meant for this movement, and what liberation could mean for women. For many early advocates of women's liberation, reform-versus-revolution confronted the elitist and racist assumptions within the demand for women's equality. Members of the women's liberation movement asked which men women wanted to be equal to, all men or white, privileged men. The first issue of *Voice of the Women's Liberation Movement (VMLM)*, Jo Freeman using the pseudonym Joreen attacks formal equality directly:

> Women's liberation does not mean equality with men. Mere equality is not enough. Equality in an unjust society is meaningless. Inequality in a just society is a contradiction in terms. We want *equality* in a *just* society. . . . As women radicals we are involved with political issues because we realize that we cannot be free until all people are free.[60] (emphases in original)

Liberation as a goal redefined what equality meant in the context of social transformation. For Benston, liberation is a site of fuller capacities to end the oppressive relations that produce women. For Firestone, liberation will lead to "the elimination . . . of the sex distinction itself."[61] The production of a just society, rather than the equal distribution of goods, is characterized by sociologist Marlene Dixon in 1970 as the difference between a demand to "let us in" and the fight to "set us free."[62] But liberation as an ideal does not explain what liberation means for that contingent group, women. In this sense, liberation is a lofty goal that defines a revolutionary movement. More specifically, as a theory about what should be, the ambitious goal of liberation has a more mundane side. That is, as a theory for political activism, a revolutionary movement for women means reformist struggles and an interdependency between revolutionary movements.

With important consequences, Benston and Joreen do not theorize the same movement, even as they both endorse its precepts of revolutionary change in women's conditions and invoke the need for reformist struggles in a revolutionary organization. Unlike Joreen's, Benston's article illustrates the contingency of movement and a lack of rigid ideological and political boundaries. In contrast, the passage cited earlier from Joreen's article in the *VWLM* presents another common understanding of less flexible distinctions. Joreen's article illustrates cross-movement relationships that secured movement boundaries, though not the women who participated in them. The political issues Joreen speaks of seem to be those struggles not within the women's liberation movement, or not immediately in the interests of women. The interdependency theorized in Joreen's article departs from Benston's less formally bounded visions of the WLM. Joreen's formulation, unlike Benston's, reiterates the boundaries that separate movements, even as she asserts their integral relationship. These two uses of movement, one which marks its perimeters, the other which refuses rigid definitions, both operated within early women's movement politics of reform-versus-revolution.

The Berkeley Women's Liberation's Wednesday Nite Group, in its discussion paper, elaborates the distinction between revolution and reform as one of larger social visions supported by reformist politics. Entitled "The Nature of Change and Political Action—Reform vs. Revolution," its paper describes the fight for day care as a goal "essential to fight for, since women cannot even be free to struggle if they are bound at home by their children."[63] Revolutionary campaigns for reforms were premised on creating the conditions necessary to build a movement for women's liberation. Position papers about women's liberation recognize struggle as reformist in these campaigns and goals. Reformist demands, they argue, fight to produce the very possibility of a women's liberation movement rather than solidify a movement-wide agenda. Day care, health care, and even economic independence are reformist goals, but they allow women to join a revolutionary movement. Still, the commitment to a revolutionary program rejects the possibility that incremental reforms can significantly change an exploitative system. If a movement's goals are limited to a single issue, any campaign can become merely reformist.[64]

Bread and Roses of Massachusetts expresses the aims of revolutionary political campaigns similarly. Equal rights are not a goal of women's liberation, but a precondition for revolutionary movement. Kathy McAfee and Myrna Wood write about a range of campaigns for equal education, equal pay, good working conditions, abortions, birth control, and the desegregation of institutions as campaigns which face "an inescapable empirical fact; women must fight their conditions just to participate in the movement."[65] Reforms are not simply a first step, but a necessary beginning for revolutionary politics. As preconditions, reformist struggles produce a political stage for feminist activists and draw women into those campaigns for political strength. Even as they build preconditions for a revolutionary movement, women struggle collectively. The object and subject of the movement blurred as the personal limits placed on women became political battles. The personal, in this vision of reform for revolution, is political.

Due to the marxist tradition of questioning the preconditions for any political aggregation, the interests of women are not wholly self-evident throughout the women's movement. Leftist theorists such as Juliet Mitchell, Clara Fraser, and Margaret Benston in the mid-sixties stress the preconditions that empower women's oppositional (both reformist and revolutionary) politics and the theoretical imperatives necessary to build a political movement defined by woman. None of these theorists set the boundaries of their inquiry in terms of the political exigencies of existing groups. Their analyses of political economy provide the means to understand conscious politics—in their possibilities, their implementation, and their trajectories.

However, as Shulamith Firestone's theory of feminist revolution illustrates, the categories woman and women can provide a fixity to the women's movement that proposals of blurred organizational affiliation to revolution cannot. Women as a class/caste system unifies all women into one struggle for liberation.[66] Women as the primary form of oppression can lead all movements. Women can reinforce the differences between movements even as they lead them together. As a unifying category, perhaps the unifying category, woman and its plural form, women, contain a presumption of political solidarity and common goals—these presumptions operate alongside contingency, diffused boundaries, and incomplete unity. Women as a category of organization in the women's liberation movement imperceptibly mutates from a site of complex socioeconomic relations and crosshatched modes of resistance/transformation into a uni-dimensional category of natural unity. These two visions competed for a movement fighting reformism as it aspired to revolution.

Reformist struggles with limited goals can be unorganized, rising from the exigencies of the moment, as well as conscious parts of organized politics. Struggle, as Luxemburg stresses, is not the same as organization, though struggle is a necessary component of organization. The women's liberation movement shed its organizational focus when all struggles became equated with organization. Firestone's popular rallying cry, "a revolutionary in every bedroom cannot fail to shake up the status quo," is one marker of this shift.[67] The slogan "The personal is political" can refer to the process that brings individual struggles, those struggles "of the bedroom," into collectively organized struggle. In Rosa Luxemburg's vision, this process strengthens both organization and unorganized struggle. But when woman is an essentialist and separatist category, the personal is political can reify individuals' struggles as the movement's totality. Firestone heralds the rise of a revolutionary movement, one stabilized by woman, and one that resides within the individual, not within the collective organization. Earlier reform-versus-revolution debates, as well as papers by theorists like Benston, remind us of our loss: a revolutionary movement that intersects with other struggles in a contingent but collective vision of feminist politics.

TWO

FEMINISM ON THE VERGE OF A NERVOUS BREAKDOWN

Chapter 1 examines early writings that suggest the historical possibility for a nonessentialist women's liberation movement. In early projections by Benston and others of a revolutionary feminist movement the analyses of the political economy of women and women's liberation imagined a contingent movement, one that responds to changing socioeconomic conditions of women. Some preconditions of this vision remain in third wave feminist writings, as it conceives of feminism as a process, not a coherent identity.[1] In this chapter, the relationship between the political economy of women and the construction of a movement is reversed. I ask how our conceptions of feminism formalized into groups and movements *produce* their subjects through assumptions about unity and dissent. The second wave women's movement celebrates its diffuse and open character, making it a slippery site for this analysis. Instead of trying to probe the movement as a whole, I will discuss one group, part of the insurgent wing of the academy, the National Women's Studies Association (NWSA). NWSA firmly locates itself within the women's movement, and seeks to bring feminist insights, methodologies, and subjects of inquiry into universities and colleges. In its early years, between 1977 and 1981, NWSA provided a creative example of how even the most committed pluralist vision of an inclusive feminism grappled to produce a diverse membership and fully representative organization.

The NWSA conference on feminism and racism, held in 1981, starkly revealed that a meaningfully plural category women did not evolve quietly in feminist discourse.[2] The struggle to define what women in feminism signifies was often as ferocious as the covert resistance to a pluralist category women. The synopses of these wide-ranging debates over the political project of feminism often center on two issues: the inclusion of diverse experiences into feminism, and an understanding of women through crosshatched relations of oppression and exploitation. Often, the issue of inclusion is reduced to a single question, remembering the outraged query to feminism: Inclusion of whom? Invocations and analyses of this question are richly explored in feminist scholarship. Feminist theory answers "inclusion of whom?"

when it locates its analytic subjects, clarifies the range of social processes at work, and most of all when it does not generalize women. Feminist theorists answer the question of inclusion in terms of the subject and subjectivity of politics. With some exceptions, feminists have forgotten its historical precedent, a question also addressed to feminism: Inclusion in what? This question opens up the site of political engagement and the movement. Just as importantly, theoretical investigations of movement and politics map the trajectories of existing political tendencies and develop alternative political models.

This chapter has two parts. First, I examine the limitations of pluralism illustrated by the 1981 NWSA conference on feminism and racism. I argue that pluralist concepts of inclusion and full representation both accommodate and undermine antiracist positions. While not necessarily individualist, pluralism privileges the subject as the site for politics. By centering on questions of the subject and subjectivity, pluralist attacks against racism shield from examination the biologically and experientially essentialist theories about feminism as a movement. Thus, pluralism preserves organizational racism in feminist politics. Second, I discuss earlier attacks against racism in feminism in writings by Francis Beale, Maryanne Weathers, and Linda LaRue. When they challenge organizational racism in feminism, these women undermine the demographic question of why black women don't join the women's movement. Rather than critique the racist feminist subject, they contest *how* the movement produces a racist collective subject through its theories about leadership, decision making, and coalitional political work. They argue that the movement must invent new techniques to nourish antiracist struggles and produce a richly diverse movement. This chapter raises their argument for further memory-work as we continue to imagine a better feminism.

Even in more recent discussions not explicitly grounded in pluralism, too often the feminist subject acts as the primary basis for understanding debates within feminism. Such essays as Linda Alcoff's "Cultural Feminism Versus Post-Structuralism: The Identity Crisis in Feminist Theory" and Deborah McDowell's "Transferences: Black Feminist Thinking: The 'Practice' of 'Theory'" continue to reinforce the conflation of the movement into its subject.[3] Both Alcoff and McDowell frame current crises faced by feminism as an ongoing negotiation between pluralism and antifoundationalism over the subject of feminism. Alcoff accepts that the subject must be the starting point for politics. She writes that "the concept and category of woman is the necessary point of departure for any feminist theory and feminist politics."[4] McDowell shows how subjects are forced to embody the divisions within feminism. Neither writer significantly reformulates the centrality of the feminist subject, nor the simplistic representation of these subjects by feminism.

For Alcoff, when woman comes into question as a homogenous, essentialist, and naturalized category, the very grounds of feminism are at stake. To destabilize woman puts the movement in jeopardy. In her analysis, until an inclusive, historicized, and fragmentary subject can endow feminist politics and feminist ethics, feminism will remain torn between pluralist empiricism and constructivist poststructuralism. Her solution, of a contingently stable feminist subject, addresses neither politics nor a movement as anything other than an outgrowth of the feminist subject.

McDowell argues that the result of this contest between an inclusive empiricism and antifoundationalism is a sexist and racist segregation of labor. Hegemonic texts in feminist scholarship create and reinforce a divide between theory and practice to manage these often-contradictory projects. White women, and white and black men carry the mantle of theory, while black women signify nontheory, or in less derogatory terms, politics/practice. McDowell writes, "(T)he strain to fulfill both requirements—to 'theorize,' on the one hand, and to recognize material 'difference,' on the other, has created a tension within academic feminist discourse (read *white*). That tension is often formulated as a contrast, if not a contest, between 'theory' and 'practice/politics,' respectively."[5] The academic production of women of color is consumed (and minimized) in this discourse as politics/practice. As a result, McDowell persuasively argues, black feminist criticism in its complexity is either marginalized or reified, and its important interventions against these silencing discourses are dismissed as undertheorized and naive. Alcoff and McDowell pinpoint aspects of a profoundly destructive essentialism in feminism. Yet the analytic centrality of the subject in politics, present in both of these discussions, produces an essentialism of its own. When they present a feminism that simply reflects the subject, they endorse a movement conceived as a collection of subjects. In this way, both writers obscure the dynamic of how feminism, as a political movement, creates and reproduces its collective subject.

Conceptually, feminist antiracist and anti-elitist invocations of inclusion suffer from their relegation to the realm of solely political interventions, devoid of theoretical insight. As a pluralist political demand, inclusion has important theoretical implications. The call for inclusion atomizes rather than collectivizes the political subject through that subject's representation by a fixed category, feminism. Feminism conceived through pluralism functions like a hologram projected by the subject in politics, without any dynamism of form or content except through these subjects. Neither widened boundaries nor contingent subjects substantively alter the centrality of the subject or the essentialism of feminism.

FEMINISM AS THE BODY POLITIC

> The National Women's Studies Association chose, as a part of the feminist movement rather than as a dutiful daughter of academia, to address the estrangement, ignorance, fear, anger, and disempowerment created by the institutional racism which saturates all our lives.[6]

Adrienne Rich delivered one of the keynote addresses at the 1981 NWSA conference, whose theme was entitled "Women Respond to Racism." She applauded the political courage of NWSA, whose conference challenged the norm of other professional women's organizations. Almost twenty years later, that conference has an iconic status in the history of women's studies. It raised difficult issues about the relation of antiracism to feminism, generated productive debates, and bared long-standing divisions between its members.

Founded in 1977, NWSA exemplifies the aspirations and contradictions of an inclusive feminism. From its founding constitution to its internal structure, NWSA stands for the ambitious project of feminist pluralist inclusion in the academy. Around NWSA cohere both the hopes and the weaknesses of pluralist redress of feminist racism. From its first convention in 1979, which nurtured the activist character of women's studies, NWSA has welcomed a wide range of issues, forums, and communication styles. Experimental in form as well as content, the association filled a need recognized as early as 1972 for a national group dedicated to women's studies.[7] For example, in 1980 NWSA formed a third world advisory council, "to involve the participation of Third World women."[8] Eight hundred letters were sent out to individuals and organizations to strengthen NWSA's efforts toward building an organization more inclusive of women of color. NWSA also reveals pluralist feminism's most glaring limitations: naturalized definitions of the movement and its subjects and fear of substantive internal dissent.

Inclusion in its colloquial form refers to a pluralist amalgamation of people, struggles, and ideologies. For the purposes of this discussion, pluralism does not just reside within the rubric of feminism, but also produces feminism as a political ideal. In other words, pluralism does not just signify an effect or product of feminist thinking but also constitutes ideologies and structures of feminism (the "politics" of feminism). Even though deeply implicated in the term *feminism,* pluralism in feminist theory defies any standardized definition. Ellen Rooney, in her insightful study *Seductive Reasoning: Pluralism in Literary Theory,* recognizes pluralism's astounding prolificacy in a wide range of disciplines and discourses.[9] Rather than overpowering other viewpoints, pluralism depends upon its discursive adaptability to produce its ubiquity.[10] The difficulty of theorizing pluralism shields its forms from scrutiny and obscures who and what benefits from its varied mobilizations.

In spite of these difficulties, Rooney locates two qualities running throughout the varied forms of pluralism that help me chart inclusion as a pluralist demand for feminists. First, pluralist discourse presumes a common mode of address: persuasion. I discuss this aspect as it shapes the language of NWSA. As the primary form of address, persuasion presumes a level field, or coequivalence between positions, that masks unequal relations of power. In this logic, all one really needs is to seek to persuade one's opponent through friendly debate, since one's views do not have materialist weight. NWSA, at its 1981 national conference, relied on these pacifying aspects of persuasion to raise the issue of racism in relation to feminism. As a result, NWSA refused to acknowledge the possibility of dissent within feminism. Rich and Audre Lorde, who addressed the conference participants, emphatically do not accede to the terms of persuasion when they celebrate dissent within the conference, women's studies, and feminism. Their celebration marks a significant break from NWSA's mobilization of persuasion. The addresses by Smith at an earlier conference, and by Lorde and Rich in 1981, forecasted the intense debate and disagreement about women and women's studies at NWSA's 1981 conference.

But the demands by the Smith, Lorde, and Rich for an ideological inclusion does not sidestep the second aspect of pluralism Rooney identifies: excluding the possibility of exclusion. Rooney describes the relation between persuasion and excluding exclusion:

> No discourse that challenges the theoretical possibility of general persuasion, no discourse that takes the process of exclusion to be necessary to the production of meaning or community and asserts, with Althusser, that it is the definition of a field which, "by excluding what it is not, makes it what it is," can function within pluralism.[11]

In the context of the challenge to NWSA by Lorde and others, the second aspect of pluralism may seem redundant. After all, Lorde et al expose the hypocrisy in the pluralist formulation of women as wholly defined by white, heterosexual, and middle-class norms. Inclusion was a rallying cry to fight the exclusion that prevailed in the women's movement and in women's studies particularly. The demand for inclusion drew attention to existing and unrecognized exclusions, in this case exclusions springing from heterosexism, elitism, and racism in the women's movement. Using a pluralist criticism of pluralism, Smith, Lorde, and Rich rely on the denial of exclusion in NWSA's pluralist discourse as an ethical wedge. They show up the hypocrisy of a pluralist movement that substantially was exclusive. But inclusion simultaneously functions as an ideal. Inclusion, in the terms of Lorde et al., once again upholds the exclusion of exclusion. The terms of inclusion harden rather than contest the givenness of women's studies and women in political solidarity. The potential contradiction of an exclusive pluralist movement, with its transformative possibilities, is thereby subverted. Even with their biting analyses of the power relations at stake in women's studies, antiracist theories by Lorde, Rich, and Smith must fall back upon a simple unity in "movement."

Feminist academic memory commonly situates critiques of feminist racism in the early eighties, particularly after the 1981 NWSA conference and the publication of such anthologies by women of color as the volume edited by Gloria Anzaldua and Cherrie Moraga, *This Bridge Called My Back* (1981), and that by Patricia Bell Scott, Barbara Smith, and Gloria Hull, *But Some of Us Are Brave* (1981). But by 1976, such journals as *Quest, Radical Teacher,* and *Conditions,* read by academic and nonacademic feminists, gave prominence to articles about feminist racism. Importantly, many of these articles did not address feminist racism alone, but linked racist exclusion to heterosexist exclusion. Their analyses forged a bond between women of color—heterosexual and lesbian—and white lesbian women in their struggle to widen feminism. By 1977, publications on issues of race and racism in feminist scholarship gained the attention of more widely distributed academic feminist journals such as *Signs* and *Feminist Studies.*

Even these debates, however, cannot be viewed as a point of origin for critiques of racism in the U.S. second wave women's movement. Instead, they must be understood in context, as an important set of critiques that challenged feminist racism as feminism slowly consolidated itself as a profession. Feminism in the academy promised a more secure financial base of operations than shakily financed jobs in the nonprofit sector. The growth of women's studies joined political commitments to an occupation. Political as well as economic concerns fueled antiracist interventions since feminist racism threatened to shut out black women and women of color from this hard-won legitimacy. With these heightened stakes, the charge of racism more than any other charge galvanized feminists in the academy to rethink their assumptions about a discipline defined by woman, and in turn to challenge the analytic category woman itself.[12] Because of women's studies' close identification with the women's movement, the repercussions of these debates have spread beyond the purview of universities and colleges. NWSA's constitution shows that the national organization for women's studies grew out of these debates. Antiracism, in NWSA's analysis, is not a corollary to feminist struggle, but is constitutive to feminism's, and by extension, the mandate of women's studies.

NWSA conceptualized itself as a mediating group between grassroots feminist activism and the academy. Through its yearly national conferences and regional meetings, NWSA proposed to provide a forum to strategize how the discipline of women's studies could build progressive institutional support for the women's movement. The group fought to bring together diverse interests within feminism, to build disciplinary guidelines for feminist scholarship, women's studies programs, and feminist scholars. In this sense, NWSA was the primary site to make feminism within the academy accountable to the demands of the women's movement.

The term *women's studies* in the group's name was visionary even in 1977, when the numbers of women's studies programs in colleges and universities were growing rapidly. Although the formation of programs flourished, funding for these programs was "soft," often reinstated on a yearly basis. Questions of adequate classes, professors, and institutional resources for women's studies were by no means settled. As a discipline, women's studies, largely on principle, did not have canonical texts, nor a common mode of analysis. Volumes of essays such as Rayna Reiter's *Toward an Anthropology of Women* and Berenice A. Carroll's *Liberating Women's History,* and Ann Gordon, Mari Jo Buhle, and Nancy Schrom Dye's pamphlet *Women in American Society,* gave direction and shape to feminist battles over how to change male bias in such disciplines as history and anthropology.[13] In addition, these texts sought to develop trajectories of analysis in feminist scholarship. Neither women's studies within the university, nor its content or methodologies as a discipline, had programmatic or structural permanence in the mid-seventies. NWSA took a leap of faith in its very name.

NWSA was formed in 1977 without the blinders of what Elizabeth Spelman calls an "additive analysis" in relation to class, race, and gender.[14] That is, NWSA did not merely invite members of color to join the organization, proclaiming its open nature. Nor did it take this invitation one step further and try to add people of color to signify or literally to represent the ideal of diversity. Nor did NWSA rest with a cursory mention in its constitution of the importance of class, sexuality, and race to feminism. NWSA proposed a pluralism which saw inclusion as a first step toward qualitatively changing feminist goals, practices, and structures. NWSA's literature focuses on women's studies as one project intimately connected to a larger movement for social change. Importantly, NWSA established an ideological rather than a demographic basis for pluralist feminism. NWSA's 1977 constitutional preamble states: "Women's studies, diverse as its components are, has at its best shared a vision of a world free not only from sexism but also from racism, class-bias, ageism, heterosexual bias."[15] This quotation illustrates NWSA's pluralist commitment to fight many forms of oppression and exploitation that affect women and men. NWSA names specific forms of bias to clarify its primary battles. Pluralism in NWSA's preamble disrupts the coequivalence between the myriad struggles waged within the women's movement. Unlike the colloquial definition of pluralism as an ideology which refuses to weigh the relative significance between things, NWSA's mandate was not a catch-all for every issue facing women. NWSA chose its battles and chose its sides. Importantly, its constitution defines NWSA's diversity through feminist struggles for freedom, not through the demographic characteristics of its proposed membership. NWSA, therefore, represented the politics of its members, rather than members' embodied interests defined through gender combined with race and class. NWSA's politics were not biologically or experientially essentialist as defined by the preamble, since NWSA's entire constituency must share a commitment to fight racism and elitism as well as sexism. In addition, the wording of this passage suggests somewhat elliptically that political differences also attend diversity in women's studies, if only by stressing the politics these components share.

NWSA held its first national convention in 1979. The response far exceeded expectation, and more than 1,100 people attended. Likewise, in 1980 a crowd of over 1,500 people joined to discuss a range of issues facing women's studies programs and departments. While the numbers of attendees were consistently higher than expected, organizers noted with some dismay that even at the second convention very few women of color participated. In 1979, panels such as "Lesbian Feminist Projects in the Community" and Margaret Simons's "Racism and Feminism: A Critique of Feminist Theory" raised issues of race and racism. Also, at the opening conference in 1980, Barbara Smith gave her frankly critical speech, "Racism and Women's Studies," which was subsequently published and republished. Smith jarred any complaisance about the goals and structures operating in women's studies as a field. She describes her vision of feminism: "(F)eminism is the political theory and practice that struggles to free *all* women. . . . Anything less than this vision of total freedom is not feminism, but merely female self-aggrandizement."[16] While talks and panels such as these gave prominence to critiques of racism and heterosexism in feminism, the actual numbers of attenders who were not white were negligible. In one report on the 1979 conference, planners noted that 93 percent of all registered conference-goers were white.[17] In 1980 that number registered a minuscule drop, to 92 percent white.[18] As these reports show, the demographic problems of building an inclusive group did not disappear with NWSA's more sophisticated rendering of its political project. Neither did its stated politics necessarily draw a racially diverse membership.

In her exhaustively researched overview of women's studies through the early eighties, Marilyn Boxer notes that concerns over the small numbers of women of color at the NWSA conference were a primary reason for the 1981 conference theme of women responding to racism.[19] NWSA took an overtly political stance by addressing the relations of racism rather than the abstract category 'race'. Their conference title signifies an almost idealistic and certainly naive project to welcome the fight against racism into the politics of feminism. When Norma Cobbs and Pat Miller announced the convention focus, they envisioned a forum to strengthen feminist antiracism, expand research on international women and women of color in the United States, and build connections between women's studies and black studies. NWSA's convention goals did not minimize differences between women, but sought to use these differences as a means to draw together disparate parts of feminism. Cobbs and Miller describe their plans to "emphasize the links, actual and potential, among cultures, among disciplines, between the educational establishment and community organizations, and between the ability to define knowledge and the ability to secure and maintain power."[20] They reiterate that the convention would move toward rectifying NWSA's inadequate attention to racism. Only one of the many proposed convention sessions ("Deliberate and Unconscious Omissions in Research") mentions problems within women's studies. Racism is not minimized in Cobbs and Miller's proposals, but they underestimate the frustration of NWSA membership toward the endemic racism within the women's movement.

The title of the conference, "Women Respond to Racism," contradicts the language of NWSA's constitution. The assumptions behind the word *respond* are twofold. First, the verb carries a tacit description of racism's location. Racism is a problem feminists must respond to, something that exists outside of women's studies, and almost certainly outside of women. Second, respond implies a nonconfrontational, almost conversational, relationship of women to racism. The bitter struggle against racism becomes, in this title, a matter of what Ellen Rooney calls "persuasion." Persuasion, as pluralism's central mode of address, deflates the opposition between positions at stake and assumes that differences can be resolved, that opponents can be persuaded to agree. Persuasion, as the terrain for pluralist politics, masks the political interests in conflict and the relations governing their production and reiteration. The conference title drains its antiracist position of its specificity and force since the language muddies who and what to confront. The diversity presumed in the conference title belies any possible political confrontation within the group's constituency or among the conference participants. Racism neither exists within their category women nor requires discussion of intraorganizational struggles. Women in this framework is not problematized by the addition of racism; instead, the term refers to a unified sociopolitical body. Because racism is viewed as external to the category women, dissent is not only minimized, but solely directed by women against racism. The absence of any recognition of internal dissent within women's studies in general or

NWSA in particular is an important lapse in a highly contentious conference. Even with a nonadditive approach to feminist inclusion, NWSA's reliance on pluralism blocked their ability to prefigure, let alone welcome or draw strength from, internal dissent.

Articles by conference organizers after the event, perhaps not surprisingly, express a tone of hurt surprise at the bitterness raised by the topic of racism. One conference participant wonders how NWSA could receive the brunt of criticisms about feminist racism, particularly since the Berkshire Women's History Conference held that year was untouched by accusations of racism even though, or because, it made no attempt to recognize racism as a central concern.[21] Some participants of the NWSA conference in 1981, however, anticipated the dissension raised by the conference theme. The opening addresses of Adrienne Rich and Audre Lorde, as well as the performance comments by Bernice Reagon of Sweet Honey in the Rock, champion the conflict that erupted at the conference as a vital and regenerative process for NWSA, women's studies, and feminism. At different points in the conference, they hail the courage of NWSA in facing feminist racism and sponsoring a possibly fracturing debate out of its commitment to diversity. These two reactions before the commencement of the conference—denial and anticipation of dissent—took other forms as the conference unfolded. Denial became suppression of dissent and anticipation turned into a celebration of dissent.

NWSA successfully opened its doors to a more racially diverse group of participants than in the previous two national conferences by hosting a conference centered on racism and women's studies. However, as Adrienne Rich suggests in her opening speech, and later statistics confirm, far fewer women attended the conference on racism than attended the previous two conferences. In fact, Deborah Rosenfelt reports that there were two-thirds fewer participants than at the conference in 1980—in other words, as many as a thousand people less than there had been the year before.[22]

Articles written after the event reiterate, from varying perspectives, several aspects of the conference.[23] All participants were assigned to consciousness-raising (CR) groups, initially on the basis of race. White women were then allowed to choose more specific topics or identifications, while third, world women were broken into smaller-sized groups, not specified by a topic, issue, or further identification. The NWSA report on the conference describes the lack of further designations for "third world women" as a an impetus for these women to decide themselves how they wanted to split up. Another report suggests that these more specific designations within the larger group of third world women were never initiated nor discussed. While initially a sore point for many women, some reports set forth the strength and insight these segregated groups produced, particularly the groups for third world women. Debates in panels and events are marked by anger, confrontation, and accusation. NWSA's report records two primary responses to the intraconference dissent. The first position supports as healthy the dissension exposed by the conference topic of racism. The second position emphasizes the external threat to the women's movement posed by the New Right.

Internal disagreement, in the second view, dissipates the urgently needed unity within the women's movement. Without a clear consensus, the women's movement cannot effectively fight the entrenched opposition to women's studies, feminism, and the women's movement. According to this view, dissent between women, even over its academic project as women's studies, threatens the women's movement as a whole and should be discouraged in favor of a strategic unity. Rosenfelt's report on the 1981 conference most clearly identifies the centrality of this position within the conference.

Earlier descriptions of NWSA conferences allude to other means used (however selectively) to suppress dissent. For example, Nancy Polikoff records how disagreements in 1980 over the proposed conference theme are couched in the language of instrumental problems. She writes, "[T]hese included, rather predictably, the difficulty in finding women to do workshops if the entire conference focused on racism."[24] Schultz and Sharistanian's report of the 1979 conference argues that the conference raises the following question: "[T]o what extent will it be necessary or possible for diverse constituencies within the NWSA to agree *not* to disagree to allow the Association to serve those diverse interests?"(emphasis in original)[25] The larger group, because of its inclusive mandate, acts as the major-ity constituency. This majority ideology takes precedence over a minority constituency (the fight against racism and/or homophobia). The logic of representative pluralism, of majority versus minority interests, is replicated in the ideological political program of the group. Rather than representing individuals, NWSA |represents political platforms, but the logic for stifling dissent operates as if these ideologies were individuals. Schultz and Sharistanian explicitly state the question of managing dissent as one of maintaining pluralism in the group. In a different vein, Stimpson's overview of the second convention suggests that participants' suspicion of authority was misplaced in the case of NWSA leadership.[26] Neither report wholly dismisses, however, the importance of dissenting positions within the conferences, but both deflect the onus of dissent from the group to the constituencies that dissented.

In her opening address, Rich preempts the acrimony and celebrates the controversy's potential to create a more open debate between conference participants. She suggests that any resulting friction stems from both white women's guilt and their laudable attempts to recognize rather than hide their racism, a recognition she describes as white women's "profound refusals to obey."[27] Rich's speech does not attempt to explain dissent by black and third world women, but addresses white women in the audience. She urges white women who identify with feminism to rise to the challenges of antiracism by dismissing self-protective guilt and admitting to their complicity with racism. Only through an ongoing process of listening, incorporation, and change, Rich argues, can white women embrace the profound refusal to cooperate with the terms of patriarchy and its attendant homophobia, elitism, and racism.

Lorde's keynote address for the same conference, entitled "The Uses of Anger: Women's Responding to Racism," describes the intents and reactions of both black and white women. She portrays dissent as a complex range of interactions:

But the angers of women can transform difference through insight into power. For anger between peers births change, not destruction, and the discomfort and sense of loss it often causes is not fatal, but a sign of growth.[28]

Lorde adds another element to dissent within feminism in her term *anger*. As an emotional response, a font for activism, anger fuels political positions of women and groups. While Rich attempts to identify and shape the impulses behind white women's reactions to dissent, Lorde looks to the impetus behind dissent within and outside the group/movement. Dissent in the form of anger does not have to divide women in feminism absolutely, but signifies that group/movement's transformation. Anger, she suggests, has the power to recreate the boundaries that define feminism.

The title of her speech plays on the conference theme when she changes *respond* to *responding*. She changes the theme's emphasis from a political project of NWSA/feminism against racism to the women who dare to answer racism back, and to these challenges as an ongoing (and historical) process. In her speech Lorde does not allow the conference theme's erasure of internal conflicts within women's studies to go unchallenged. But as her title illustrates, she opens a dialogue on how to reconceptualize such a conference, and voices her disagreeement without condemning the entire forum. Her speech and presence at the conference embody her distinctions between conflict within feminism and the struggles feminism wages.

The elision of dissent reflected by NWSA's 1981 conference title illustrates assumptions that infect a much wider range of demands for inclusion into feminism. For example, the arguments about feminism outlined by Rich and Lorde have significant points of agreement with NWSA's constitution. As feminist proposals advocating an inclusive feminism, these arguments build on other aspects of pluralist politics as well. Inclusion draws on the pluralist tradition of politics in the United States and carries the assumption about adequate representation *of* the subject *by* the movement. Inclusion as a demand contains an ethical charge against the movement for failing to live up to its commitments as a representational body or failing to make particular political commitments. The burden of this charge, however, is shouldered by those subjects (particularly—though by no means only—leaders) who identify themselves as part of that movement. Not only the subjects of the organization, but also their political subjectivity come under suspicion. The failure of a movement or group, whether the failure is ongoing racism or homophobia, is the fault of its members and their political-personal development. At the outset, this assumption seems fairly obvious: who else can be blamed for group/movement weaknesses? An organization, after all, is the sum of its parts and exists only because of the subjects who predicate its possibility.

Presuppositions about organization anchor both positions about the 1981 conference, whether they support or deny dissent, and whether they refer to a larger movement like the women's movement or a smaller group like NWSA. The position in support of dissent depends upon a psychological component of organization. Lorde uses the term anger to signify dissent. She writes, "[M]y response to racism is anger." The subjects of the political movement, women as a political constituency, react to structural exploitation and sociopolitical oppression with anger.

Likewise, differences within the women-constituency enact anger. Through emotive responses such as anger, guilt, and resignation, Rich and Lorde figure dissent through the subjects and subjectivities of the movement/group, and not as something embedded in political organization.

The position against dissent at the 1981 NWSA conference can be oversimplified as a cynical attempt to squelch any sustained recognition of racism in feminism. If prominence were accorded to analyses of racism and race in feminist classrooms and scholarship, scholarship that denied or ignored their importance could lose value. Scholars and activists, in this calculation of interests, would have personal economic and political reasons to drown out antiracist demands for women's studies. But there is more at stake than raw self-interest in the position against dissent. This argument reinforces the difference between inside and outside, and reestablishes the permanence of movement/group boundaries. Dissent-as-difference constitutes the movement/group's boundaries in an absolute form. If its boundaries are fixed, so too is its polity. Given these constraints, it is no wonder dissent from within is viewed with an almost paranoid suspicion, as Alcoff later argues. Disagreement between members alienates unequivocally, since unity, political solidarity, indeed, the entire structure of the group/movement is thrown into jeopardy, and the definition of who and what is outside must begin again. The goal of preserving unity demands a homogeneity: since unity is defined as agreement between members, the group/movement's polity must be eternally as one. The group/movement and the political organization that sustains it are static, preexistent, and homogenous. The group/movement acts as an amalgamation of its parts, one that simply reflects a political platform or constituency.

One position on dissent allows for political organization as a process, while the other depends upon its stasis, which it calls stability or unity. Yet both positions are grounded in common pluralist visions of the group/movement. For while dissent is seen as catastrophic to a static definition of women's studies, the celebrants of dissent refuse to elaborate on the possible dissolution or fragmentation caused by movement differences. Neither do they overtly discuss the possibility, even the necessity, of exclusion in a women's movement, since the operative word in Lorde's keynote address is *growth*. Political organization as an organic construct presumes, at some level, that the organism is whole. While boundaries in this conception are less rigid, they remain presupposed, as is the movement/group. The full range of a movement/group's organizational production is ignored. Inclusion, for advocates of positions against and in favor of dissent, is primarily concerned with the subject of politics. In both cases, the discussion of the movement/group is bounded by the exigencies of the subject in politics, and by the questions of adequate representation. In neither position does the collective form have a logic beyond the demands of political subjects and subjectivities.

Lorde and Rich couple inclusion with dissent to engender a thorough rethinking of whether diversity can support a simple pluralist vision of feminism. Their positions question whether all women can expect to join the same group or unite within the same movement. They also ask whether a wholly inclusive movement can expect to remain ideologically stable in the face of constitutive diversity. These analyses both utilize and question the fundaments of pluralist feminism. In addition, as critiques from participants positioned within feminism, they begin to question how theorists and activists conceptualize feminism. If inclusion denotes one basis for feminism, Lorde, Rich, Smith, and other critics of feminist racism from this period question the premises of the movement from the vantage of racism within feminism. They isolate two aspects of racist feminism for their most serious interrogation: the subjects who identify with feminism and the subjects presumed (and projected) by feminism. They ask how the project of feminism is articulated in pluralist analyses to reproduce racism in the very structures they confront. At the heart of the analyses by Lorde, Smith, and Rich is the question of why inclusion does not necessarily throw feminist racism into crisis. But it was precisely around inclusion that early second wave articulations of feminist racism cohered.

MISPLACING THE SUBJECT OF FEMINIST RACISM

Feminist racism frames the exclusion of women of color as a concern about the participation of black women in feminism. The exemplary question of demographic pluralism, heard throughout the second wave women's movement, was characterized simply by one white activist in 1970: "Frequently at women's liberation meetings the question is raised, why aren't there any black sisters?"[29] In this question, the lack of black women in groups and events organized by the women's movement is recognized as a recurrent problem. The problem concerns the homogeneity of women who join the women's movement. It involves not only the homogeneity, or lack of diversity of women, but also these women's relationship to dominant power structures as white women in a racist system. The ideology and goals of the women's movement—fighting for liberation from existing relations of oppression and exploitation—make the whiteness of the movement's members a problem. Implicit in the worry about members of the women's movement was the doubt that middle-class white women, alone, would consistently fight oppression based on racism or exploitation based on elitism. The definition of the movement was also at stake. The women's movement professed to organize all women who fought for liberation or equality. The legitimacy of "women's movement," as an inclusive construct able to unite all leftist/liberal women, comes under threat if only white women are feminists. If the movement could not base those claims on a widely representative membership, then women as a political purview needed reassessment.

The answers to the question of why black women do not join the women's movement vary as widely as the women who asked it. When a problem is couched as one about (projected) subjects of the movement, the riddle of the missing black feminists is solved in two ways. One approach focuses on the women's movement as a flawed construct, unable to attract or represent a diverse category, women. In the early seventies, most commentators chose to explore the character of the movement. Some explicitly theorize the women's movement by its majority constituency of white, middle-class women.[30] Others challenge existing hierarchies of leadership and policy-making that repelled black women and reinforced the dominance of whites in the membership.[31]

The second approach focuses on the political identification of individual subjects: on the politics of black women. In this analysis, black women bear peculiar problems of political identification that prevent them from becoming feminists. Feminist racism thrived in interpretations about the political subjectivity of black women. The question, Why don't black women join the women's movement? addresses representative pluralism, or who the women's movement represents. In the early second wave women's movement, this question transgressed ideological boundaries of radical or cultural feminism. Likewise, feminist racism does not operate solely within a particular group or political agenda. Instead, the term feminist racism identifies the relationship of feminism as an ideology and as a movement to its larger structural context in a deeply racist and elitist system. Feminist racism is reproduced while simultaneously being combated. Antiracism cannot be awarded a determinate end, even within the more limited, more progressive confines of feminism, while racism binds daily social, political, and economic relations of the larger community.

Feminists posed the question of low numbers of black women within the women's movement as a paradox. The focus of inquiry is black women. The paradox lies in the disjunction between the projected membership of the women's movement (which includes black women) and its actual membership demographics, white women. That is, the paradox lies between the all-encompassing *women* of *women's movement,* and its limited realization. In this way, the question can be restated as why does women denote white women? The crisis of unity for the women's movement rests on the nonattendance of black women at events like the 1981 NWSA conference. But the question is asked in terms of black women: Why don't they come? The question posed as a paradox of black women shifts the burden from the construct women's movement to its renegade subject, black women. Effectively, this question evades asking why the women's movement does not or cannot bring together all women engaged in progressive activism. It shifts the dilemma from the movement to the subject of the movement.

Posed as a paradox, admittedly one for feminists to figure out, this question makes two assumptions: first, that woman is a homogenous category, and second that woman is a natural political constituency. In this logic, even if black women do not join the women's movement, they are part of its rightful constituency. The question assumes that black women have a natural affinity to this women's movement, in fact to any women's movement, because they are women. Women is a natural constituency through a homogenous gender oppression. Effectively then, membership precedes individual organizational affiliation. This assumption about a given membership, a membership defined by both biology and undifferentiated experience, supports a conclusion that has been explicated many times before. Black women, in this logic, are the same political constituency in the women's movement as white women. Women becomes a unified and essentialist category which collapses the subject in politics with a projected political constituency.

The antagonistic interpretation of why black women do not join the women's movement rests on a similarly presupposed definition of political subjectivity. If black women are reducible to "women," then their lack of participation rests on their own faulty political development. The numbers of black women exist, but black women have not accepted their true political affiliation. The basis for all women's political subjectivity is a given and known entity, therefore women who do not embrace their ineluctable political identity must suffer from false consciousness. Subjectivity, or the formation of political identification, emerges only as women accept the fate presaged by the movement's possessive definition of women's and join up. I am overdrawing the assumptions within these questions to lend definition to the logic supporting writings that suggest that black women will come to the movement with a little more time to consider.[32]

The quandary was heightened by a 1972 poll sponsored by Virginia Slims that showed a far greater percentage of black women than white women supported the goals of feminism and the organization of women for equal rights.[33] Taking into account this statistic, the question shifted slightly: If black women support the project of feminism, why don't they join the women's movement? Again phrased around the assumption of a derelict constituency, this question assumes two things: first, the women's movement represents the entirety of existing and potential feminist goals, and more sweepingly, feminism as a progressive or radical political analysis defined through gender *is* the women's movement. These two assumptions about the purview and the ideology of the movement are interconnected. Here, the women's movement is not conceived in context, as one formation to build solidarity and organize women, but as the *only* correct political formation for anyone subordinated due to gender relations. Ideologically, the feminist political agenda, like the women's movement, has fixed boundaries and by definition represents the interests of all women. This question assumes that all women who recognize their oppression will join the women's movement, and that the women's movement can represent them all.

In the many permutations of this question, even those eliciting sympathetic answers, the onus of a predominantly white women's movement remains on black women's subjectivity, not on the character of the women's movement.[34] Not only is the answer shifted away from one requiring collective rethinking on the part of women identifying with the women's movement, but also away from any careful analysis of what a women's movement should be. Critiques grounded in a potential constituency, in this case women of color, particularly black women, can only address the subjectivity and political identification of the subjects in question. Even if the blame is shifted from potential members to white feminists who identify as members of the women's movement, the individual's political subjectivity is still at the fore, as in the question, Why don't activist white women create a more racially diverse women's movement? The focus of this question is still on the politics of how these individuals represent themselves in their political activism, rather than how they represent their group/movement. A simple reversal of feminist racist logic, which switches the blame to white women, remains at the level of the particular subject in politics. This methodological individualism is a distinguishing feature of feminist racism, and has wide-reaching consequences. The processes and structures of the movement remain hidden from scrutiny. At the center of feminist racism is a stubborn refusal to theorize organization; instead, the foundations of feminist racism depend upon the biologically and experientially anchored categories of political organization. Feminist racism shifts the criticism for racial discrimination in the women's movement from political organization, particularly the (re)production of the group/movement, to the individual black or white woman and the collective subject, black and white women.

The hard-hitting critiques of Lorde and Rich, while vital to retheorizing the subject of feminist politics, do not confront the organizational myopia of feminist racism. The terms of pluralism, with its focus on the subject in politics, do not lead to a thorough recognition of the production of movement. Rather, pluralist frameworks of inclusion and full representation view the movement through the exigencies of the subject alone. Lorde and Rich denaturalize the presumed subject of feminism, they question the scope of feminism, and they complicate simplistic assumptions about political subjectivity. However, they only confront the terms of the movement through the subject. They leave alone the production of politics and the dynamic of existing mechanisms guiding politics, with the significant exception of how politics produces the subject of feminism. Organization, as the intersection between theory and practice, only emerges in the subject, not in the movement. As a naturalized construct, movement is wrenched from its ideological production (theory) and represents pure practice, unaccountable to history. Due to their methodological individualism, Lorde and Rich confront feminist racism largely within the parameters set by feminist racist discourse.

Feminist political identification and the production of a women's movement were never ignored, particularly in the very early stages of the second wave women's movement. Black, Asian, Native American and Latina women who were active in a range of political organizations and movements responded sharply to the insinuation that women of color were at fault for their small numbers in the women's movement.[35] Black, Asian, Latina, and white women, heterosexual and lesbian, posed (or answered) the question of why the women's movement was predominantly white and middle class.[36] In the late sixties and early seventies, unlike in the late seventies, criticisms of feminist racism are not grounded in pluralism. Usually informed by a marxist or left-nationalist analysis, these critiques direct their attacks against political organization in the women's movement. That is, they contest the presumptions of the term movement more than those of the term of women. These activists target poor political platforms, leadership structures that maintained discrimination against black and working-class women, separatism from other progressive movements, and elitist campaigns.

In 1969, Frances M. Beale of SNCC's Black Women's Liberation Committee wrote the enormously influential paper "Double Jeopardy: To Be Black and Female," published in many feminist anthologies from the early seventies. Importantly, she denounces trends in the women's movement even as that movement struggled to take shape. She writes:

> If the white groups do not realize that they are in fact fighting capitalism and racism, we do not have common bonds. If they do not realize that the reasons for their condition lie in the system . . . then we cannot unite with them around common grievances or even discuss these groups in a serious manner because they're completely irrelevant to the black struggle.[37]

Beale questions the potential opportunism of this new movement, which denounced racism and gained legitimacy from the dynamic civil rights and Black Power movements of the late sixties. In dismay, she notes the often simplistic connections drawn between the struggles of white and black women in the name of sisterhood. Beale argues that the women's movement cannot simply rest its assertions of cross-race and cross-class solidarity, whether between women or movements, to create political unity, or even its own political possibility.

Instead, Beale judges the politics of the women's movement by that movement's understanding of sexism in the context of racism and capitalism. The relations of racism and capitalism, Beale states, likewise must define the movement's purview (women) in order to produce a substantive antiracist commitment. Without an analysis of women sensitive to issues of race and class, she suggests, the solidarity of the women's movement with antiracist struggles was merely window dressing. In her essay, Beale presents the possibility of betrayal of the civil rights movement by the women's movement, due to weak theoretical foundations guiding the latter movement's political commitments. She judges the movement on its own terms, given its projection of itself as a movement of liberation.

In step with numerous other critics of the growing movement, she does not concentrate on individual racists lodged within feminist groups. Challenges like Beale's counsel for better political organization uncover the myopia and racism that are also part of this women's movement. Beale locates an ideological and programmatic basis for a divergence between organizing black and white women, which radically affects how the movement would develop. Groups like Black and Third World Women's Liberation in Cambridge, Massachusetts, and Women in Action in New York City also proposed the transformation of leadership roles, decision-making channels, unity, and coalition building to support antiracism and antielitism in the women's movement and in organizing techniques more generally. Rich with suggestions of other ways to organize women, these critiques oppose the racism endemic to women's movement groups and campaigns in their suggestions for alternate practices. But as structural critiques of the movement in the United States, they charge the women's movement not with personal racism, but organizational racism: a racism snared within the structures and assumptions guiding the movement. Feminist racism did not go unchecked; in fact, feminist racism developed alongside (and in constant confrontation with) the vibrant and informed antiracist political activism of the late sixties and early seventies.

Probably the most potent, and unanswered, suggestion for the redefinition of women's movement in the United States came around the issue of leadership, to combat the tyranny of the majority. In the heady spirit of self-determination and the fight for third world national independence from colonial rule, leadership in movements for liberation in the United States marked a critical site for building a different women's movement. In addition, leadership issues involved questions about the relative autonomy of groups within (and intersecting) movements, as a means to dispel the movement's reiteration of the dominant power relations. Participants grappled with issues of group/movement leadership, and an increasingly complex redefinition of group boundaries and political alliances, trying to restructure simplistic conceptions about group interests and group representation of its membership. Linda La Rue was one of many analysts in the early seventies who turned the question of racism-versus-sexism inside out when she posed the importance of women's liberation to the ongoing struggle against racism.[38] She argues that the existing women's movement would diverge further from the struggle against racism and capitalism as the movement reached more and more white, middle-class women.[39] To combat this trajectory, she outlines the importance (for the goals of Black liberation) of black women's active participation in women's liberation. She writes:

> Though most white women's lib advocates fail to realize the possibility, their subsequent liberation may spell a strengthening of the status quo values from which they sought liberation. Since more and more women will be participating in the decision making process, those few women participating in the "struggle" will be outnumbered by the more traditional middle class women.[40]

Increasing the numbers of black women fighting for a militantly antiracist women's liberation will not sway the movement's turn from antiracism, she argues, but an informed support for the women's liberation movement by the black liberation movement could. Leadership, in La Rue's conception, is neither top-down nor bottom-up, in any strict sense. Neither does she propose that black women are the vanguard force to lead all women. Instead, La Rue's analysis depends upon the flexibility of the women's movement, even as she outlines its ongoing dynamic. She relies not on exceptional leaders, but on a careful theory of the movement defined by women, to transform the disturbing trends she foresees. Activism, in both Beale's and La Rue's conceptions, depends upon theorizing the movement in its context to shape women as a site for political struggle.

The complexity of La Rue's and Beale's interventions in the production of the women's movement lends another dimension to answering the queries about racism in women's studies. Their positions demand that we articulate the limits of the movement/group/discipline at hand, and the possible scope of that particular site of feminist politics. Beale and La Rue project other trajectories for the women's liberation movement, such as impoverished theories of liberation, and political agendas that uphold existing relations of power. They draw their alternatives from their analyses of what the movement is and where it is going, but they do not assume those disturbing trajectories are predestined, or effectively *are* the movement. Both Beale and La Rue transform the question of feminist racism, in their methodology and conclusions. Beale answers what kind of women's movement black women should join. La Rue shifts the terms further when she projects the kind of women's movement black *people* and black movements can produce.

Theorists of feminism must constantly negotiate and make explicit those boundaries of gender, race, sexuality, and class which seem to preexist or, in the case of second wave feminism, determine a movement. These prescriptions for constantly negotiated boundaries are, by now, dominant in studies of the women's movement and feminism. Histories of women's activism have looked well beyond the groups which called themselves feminist, and issues presumed to be women's issues.[41] But even as we chart those groups, texts, and campaigns that complicate simplistic definitions of feminism, we must uncover the theories that intersect that practice. Without this analysis of organization, the terms of the movement and the assumptions about politics do not surface, and the theory/practice divide so compellingly analyzed by McDowell endures. Feminism becomes wider, more diverse, but its production and reproduction remain naturalized.

Importantly, the terms exclusion and inclusion present within NWSA and antiracist critiques of the late seventies and early eighties also invoke the movement's boundaries, asking what lies within and without feminism. As a transformative prescription for the movement, inclusion contains a charge to take stock of the movement's boundaries and provide an explicit clarification of what constitutes its political terrain, women. The demand for inclusion of women of color and lesbian women into the U.S. women's movement, since its early articulations in the mid-seventies, contain both questions—who is included and what can include them. As critiques of the subject and subjectivity, the works of Audre Lorde, Adrienne Rich, and Barbara Smith, among others, force the reconceptualization of feminism, but only through an organic conception of feminism as a kind of extension of the subject in politics. Racist theories of feminism turn inclusion into an intensely personal attack against that pluralistic group, women, outside of feminism. Much more vehemently than antiracist theories of inclusion, feminism is impervious to criticism, above the fray of flawed political individuals. The blinders that racist feminism places on the production of movement and politics have direct implications for the power of inclusion as a counterstrategy.

In this essay, NWSA bears heavy responsibility for the failure of pluralist strategies to resolve feminist racism. But as we must bear in mind, the fact that NWSA attempted to address feminist racism at all is a radical departure from other university groups and conferences defined by the category women. Likewise, to blame the challenges NWSA faced and continues to face structured by pluralism oversimplifies its other legacies of struggle. Rather than untangle these complicated historical threads, this essay concentrates on how the problems of feminism were framed by pluralism. In contrast, the earlier fight by Beale and others against organizational racism condemns racism intrinsic to the production and reproduction of feminism as a theory and as a movement. NWSA, through the committed intervention of people such as Lorde and Rich, paid careful attention to feminism's subjects and subjectivities. However, NWSA only regarded the movement as a function of those subjects, therefore racism and antiracism revolved around the subject. For this reason, critiques of feminist racism could not address racism as it produced women and feminism organizationally.

THREE

THE TYRANNY OF POSTSTRUCTURELESSNESS

Attempts to control or refuse dissent within a group, as NWSA's early debates around their antiracist commitments illustrate, rarely sustain political unity. Without a means for participants to disagree, the boundaries of a movement or group rigidify or collapse. Perhaps, then, the more recent move in the nineties to support all dissent all the time attends to these lessons. But this unqualified celebration of dissent, particularly present in postfoundationalist arguments about feminism, rests on a rejection of organization as an inherently coercive imposition. Dissent disbands any long-term invocation of unity, while ephemeral forms like the coalitional assemblage attempt to give organizational form to this profoundly antiorganizational vision. These arguments span the second wave women's movement, however, as proponents in the early seventies of 'structurelessness' tried to oppose hierarchy through a lack of group structure via consciousness-raising groups. This chapter explores how organizational forms, like the consciousness-raising group and coalitional assemblage, are embedded in contemporary feminist theory.

Critics denounce postfoundationalist arguments about feminism as lacking commitment to progressive, or more specifically Leftist, politics.[1] For some, postfoundationalist questions about a reified subject of feminist politics dismantle any grounds for political engagement.[2] Essentialism, in this critique, is not merely strategic but an important basis for political organization around woman. In this essay, I draw a different conclusion about the character of postfoundationalist feminism. Even those antiessentialist positions that say very little about activism or politics, respond explicitly to feminist theories about politics. Much has been written about Judith Butler's politics of performativity, but Butler's, Diana Fuss's, and Donna Haraway's writings illustrate how the contingent subject of postfoundationalism also informs their arguments about feminism as a movement.[3] In many aspects, the nonfoundationalist subject mirrors the form of political organization they propose. As that contingent subject has a shifting character, so too should political struggles resist any formalization into a political organization.

Antiessentialist arguments about feminism attack political organization, not politics. Antiorganizational positions defining feminism, such as Fuss's and Haraway's, have a longer tradition than the emergence of poststructuralism or postmodernism within the academy. Antiorganizational arguments challenging the formalization of politics in second wave feminism have been traced to arguments for participatory democracy in groups such as the Students for a Democratic Society (SDS), the Student Non-Violent Coordinating Committee (SNCC), the Congress of Racial Equality (CORE), and others.[4] Early in the second wave women's movement, the slogan "the personal is political" embodied a central strategy to counter women's marginalization in student movements against the Vietnam war, imperialism, and the draft.[5] Yet this slogan provided one focus for the development of antiorganizational theories particular to the conditions of feminism.

Judith Butler, in *Gender Trouble,* promotes an unqualified support for dissent, which I am calling "struggle," both within feminism and around women. Her discussion of dissent also outlines the contingent subject of politics, and the contours of politics for postfoundationalism. She conceives of struggle as a process, a series of contestations and rearticulations around an infinitude of differences which shape and reshape feminism. Struggle, as it produces and reproduces the subject, is the primary dynamic for a postfoundationalist feminist politics. I discuss works by Haraway and by Gayatri Spivak, as well as by Butler, to explore who or what struggles in postfoundationalist arguments about feminism.[6]

On the basis of a critique of a universalist subject, Rosemary Hennessey and Teresa de Lauretis both stress the similarities between the visions of antiracist feminists and antifoundationalist feminists.[7] In her book, *Materialist Feminism and the Politics of Discourse,* Hennessey argues for an analytic and political category, 'materialist feminism', to reflect the strong connection between antiracist and antiessentialist theories about feminism. She writes:

> Over the past twenty years, the voices of women who have found themselves outside the boundaries of that mainstream—women of color, lesbians, working class, and "third world" women—have pressured feminism to question the adequacy of a generic "woman" and gender-centered feminist inquiry.[8]

Hennessey correctly locates the close correlation between a specifically antiracist critique of exclusion and the struggle against feminist homophobia and class-bias. She clearly marks the political terrain of arguments for inclusion within feminism to construct an alliance between a postfoundationalist distrust of unity and antiracist fight to redefine feminism.

Both antiracist and postfoundationalist arguments about feminism encourage and respect the value of dissent within a movement or group. Rather than smother dissent with a universal feminism, antiracists and postfoundationalists argue that feminism can only strengthen its political commitments through constant reassessment and revision of its weaknesses.[9] Writers such as Judith Butler openly affirm the importance of disagreement between feminists. As Butler writes, "[R]ifts among women . . . ought to be safeguarded and prized."[10] Rather than accommodating all feminists, the struggle over feminist racism, Butler contends, helps to define political differences between women and feminisms.

The common bond between antiracist and postfoundationalist arguments in support of dissent within feminism weakens, however, when they address political organization. Antiracist, socialist, marxist, and postcolonial views of feminism combine a commitment to dissent within feminism with a firm support for the political organization either with, for, or by women. For this reason, the antiracist feminist critique of a universal category woman cannot be generalized as just another critique of totality. Unlike antiracist critiques, the celebration of dissent in postfoundationalist writings does not advocate structural changes or modifications in the political organization of feminism. Rather, struggle heralds the project to dismantle political organization itself.

The telling feature of postfoundationalist and postmodernist feminist analyses is not their critique of a feminist subject, but how they theorize this subject's relationship to political organization. Postfoundationalists' trademark skepticism of feminist unity and structure is just the most recent articulation of antiorganizational positions.[11] In the late sixties, the slogan "the personal is political" did not signify one organizational form or even one theory of feminist politics.[12] But by the early seventies, the consciousness-raising group was a primary site for experiments with leaderless and structureless organizational forms—one that accommodated internal dissent through their proliferation. The memory-work I undertake in this chapter draws on recent and past assessments, and suggests potential weaknesses of unaccountable and de facto leadership for postfoundational theories about politics.

POSTFOUNDATIONALIST STRUGGLE

Butler, Haraway, Spivak, and other postfoundationalist theorists seriously question any humanist subject for feminism, but not at the expense of feminist political engagement. They do not shy away entirely from humanism, though they limit its statute to the realm of politics alone. The contingent subject of antiessentialist feminist politics answers the demands of politics for agency and an agent. In light of its evanescent and strategic quality, this contingent subject seems poorly equipped to carry the full weight of postfoundationalist politics. To understand what the anti-essentialist subject means for feminism as a political entity, I will begin with its central critique of humanist feminism against naturalized categories of sex and of gender.

Politics in postfoundationalism are not merely discursive (a term that sometimes stands in for nonmaterial), as some critics have charged, but they are discursively determined in the last instance. Politics operate in the interstices of subject formation, a process which is always contestatory and never given. Due to the relations of discursive production, or inscription, the subject is always political. But postfoundationalism also allows for an overtly political subject—what I call a "contingent subject." This contingent subject can consciously intervene in and attempt to subvert its own hegemonic discursive formation.[13] The fight for contingency, waged by this political subject, can make visible often unrecognized processes and relations of power at work. These politics expose normative definitions of the subject which attempt to erase the conditions of its construction. Butler describes the importance of understanding bodies' materiality: "[We] are not merely considering how bodies appear from the vantage point of a theoretical position . . . we are asking how the criteria of intelligible sex operates to constitute a field of bodies, and how precisely we might understand specific criteria to produce the bodies that they regulate."[14] A contingent subject, in postfoundationalist models, can hope at best to undermine any fixity in its signification, and thus subvert the relations of power which produce and reinforce its meaning. Politics, in this discursive realm, remain largely at the level of dissent or opposition rather than transformation, since the contingent subject is a political actor by virtue of never actually becoming.

In her discussion of Butler, Pheng Cheah argues that performative politics presume a very specific set of conditions. Cheah writes that the battle to resignify the body is partly "based on the tacit presupposition of an established culture of democratic contestation within the constitutional nation-state form."[15] I would take Cheah's argument a step further, because in this system, determined in the last instance by hegemonic relations of signification, any flexibility of contingency must travel the well-worn tracks of power and capital. Politics are not collective in their subjects, their expressions of agency, nor in their goals, and can only contest repressive discursive relations on their own terms. Postfoundational politics, theorized through the subject and suspicious of any relations of power and collective politics, are not exactly antifeminist. They are, however, antiorganizational: they are defined by contingency, and fight any remnants of formal political organization.

For Judith Butler, politics play out between the subject's gendered identification (or the subject's negotiation with gendered identification) and normative definitions of absolute sexual difference.[16] Butler writes about the political subversion of a stable identity:

> Inasmuch as "identity" is assured through the stabilizing concepts of sex, gender, and sexuality, the very notion of "the person" is called into question by the cultural emergence of those "incoherent" or "discontinuous" gendered beings who appear to be personal but who fail to conform to the gendered norms of cultural intelligibility by which persons are defined.[17]

Butler calls this self-conscious process of identification a subject's "identity." The antiessentialist discursive identity constantly negotiates and is negotiated within a political sphere of relations. Emancipatory politics, for Butler, lie somewhere between the overwhelming structures of power that define the limits of sexual difference and the negotiation of those limits by nonconforming or incoherent subjects. She suggests that identity cannot be wrested away through alternate meanings or names, but only through contesting the very grounds that name and pinpoint identity. While Butler extols the liberating possibilities of identities which never close or stabilize, this unstable subject-in-politics poses serious difficulties for any definition of a self-conscious political actor or even conscious politics.[18] Effectively, Butler's discursive subject of politics undermines any definitive demarcation between political and apolitical. Since the negotiations of meaning construct and deconstruct the conditions for an identity's political involvement, the process of the subject's discursive construction itself is political. Displacement (of gender, sexual difference, identity) is not one goal of feminism, it is feminist political practice.

This reiteration of the political qualities within the subject for feminist politics, or a feminist identity, creates a crisis of meaning. If the subject of feminism is political it follows that the processes by which this subject is negotiated are politics. As Amanda Anderson points out in her essay discussing poststructuralism, this too is a limited definition of politics. "To conceive of the subject as a participant in its own constructions, however is not the same as conceiving of the subject in social communities. The self-disciplining, self-inscribing, or self-parodic subject is one whose most fundamental relation is to the system and not to other subjects."[19] Conceptually, the subject in Butler's politics must operate in isolation from other parodies, other subversions of hegemonic power relations. The protesting subject, even if acting in concert with other subjects, is not transformed or even qualified for being part of a group. One answer to my opening question about who or what struggles in postfoundationalist arguments, then, is the contingent politicized subject, or identity—a subject that struggles simultaneously as both the object and subject of politics. Butler does not foreclose the potential for a subject's politics to affect its discursive construction through language. However, Butler theorizes the subject as an enclosed system; thus, the subject of Butler's politics is only theorized at an atomized level.

Gayatri Spivak develops an argument against those politics that begin with the collective and essentialist subject.[20] She attempts to delink the humanist subject from a collective subject in politics. Spivak builds on Denise Riley's book about a contingent category, woman, when she articulates an early position now called "strategic positivist essentialism" or just "strategic essentialism."[21] Linked explicitly to the demands of political collectivities, strategic essentialism allows for a transgression into essentialism in order to consciously build political identification between subjects engaged in politics.[22] Spivak defined the term in her essay about Indian historiography, "Subaltern Studies: Deconstructing Historiography." Just as some feminist scholarly projects that write *woman* as the subject of inquiry, Subaltern Studies fought to constitute Indian history through the problematic of subaltern consciousness. Spivak describes the project of Subaltern Studies as "a *strategic* use of positivist essentialism in a scrupulously visible political interest."[23] She further elaborates her concept through class consciousness as both a descriptive and transformative category. The descriptive term is used strategically to produce the conditions for its transformative potential.[24] The transformation of class through class consciousness demands a self-alienating category; a category which potentially demolishes or deconstructs itself. Politics for Spivak very explicitly depend upon a collective relationship between subjects. In this sense, they allow that the exigencies of collective politics demand some recognition of essentialism in relation to the political subject.

Spivak's argument for a "scrupulously visible," or self-conscious strategic essentialism, only opens the door for a discussion of what a collective consciousness entails. Curiously absent in Spivak's endorsement of political organization are the means by which this essentialism will ultimately self-deconstruct. While strategic essentialism invokes collective will, Spivak places emphasis primarily on the subject rather than on organization. Even as a collectivity, the subject of politics never departs from the terrain of its discursive construction. In this sense, Spivak remains much truer to the tradition of antiessentialist arguments about feminism since she stays at the level of the subject's relationship to politics, or how subject formation is political.

Donna Haraway's essay "A Cyborg Manifesto: Science, Technology, and Socialist-Feminism in the Late Twentieth Century" provides an evocative illustration of how antiessentialism guides the political organization of feminism.[25] The antiessentialist cyborgian subject of politics never invokes basic unities or timeless essences. Instead, cyborgs provide an intersection between animal, human, and machine for fragmentary coalitions. Feminism, as constituted through political organization, is marked by unexpected combinations of interests, and intimate contradictions of space and power relations. The metaphor of coalitions facilitates Haraway's vision:

> Ironically, it might be the unnatural cyborg women making chips in Asia and spiral dancing in Santa Rita jail whose constructed unities will guide effective oppositional strategies. . . . I like to imagine LAG, the Livermore Action Group, as a kind of cyborg society . . . committed to building a political form that actually manages to hold together witches, engineers, elders, perverts, Christians, mothers, and Leninists long enough to disarm the state.[26]

Haraway describes momentary coalitions forged through members' choice-based affinity, to form a noncoercive political organization. While her proposal is unlike Butler's or Spivak's, Haraway is still deeply committed to fighting any endorsement of feminist political essentialism.[27] Haraway theorizes political identities in the trajectory laid out by Spivak, through those political formations which will deconstruct themselves. Likewise, political collectivities can only "hold together . . . long enough" to realize a proposed goal, however farsighted. Haraway admits that collectivities are instrumental to politics, but she does not merit them with careful theoretical attention. As temporary collections of contingent subjects, the collective subject of politics must be constantly undermined and, reformed to produce an antiessentialist vision of feminist political organization. Like Butler's, Haraway's politics more closely resemble dissent or opposition than transformation.

The simultaneous enabling and disrupting of affinity coalitions are the pre-condition for Haraway's politics. She invokes Adrienne Rich and critiques her po-sition: "The feminist dream of a common language, like all dreams for a perfectly true language, of perfectly faithful naming experience, is a totalizing and imperi-alist one."[28] These affinity coalitions dissipate presumably in order to renew other affiliations in endlessly multiple connections. Again, the cyborgian subject, how-ever internally fragmented, is the unit through which these collectivities build. Har-away concentrates on the integrity of the antiessentialist subject/cyborg in politics. She simply mirrors the fragmentary, changing articulations of this antiessentialist subject in the organizational form of shifting, internally contradictory coalitions. Without the organization, Haraway imagines that oppositional politics can un-dermine a return of imperialism in any guise. Precisely because these formations re-sist political organization, she suggests, the coercive relations of power cannot reestablish themselves. Again, politics and power are closely and dangerously linked in postfoundationalist positions.

Butler asserts a similar stance when she describes antiessentialist coalitions in feminism as strictly against unity. She states; "This anti-foundationalist approach to coalitional politics assumes neither that 'identity' is a premise nor that the shape or meaning of coalitional assemblage can be known prior to its achieve-ment."[29] Butler argues that feminists must embrace internal contradictions as part of the process of politics. Dissent, in Haraway's and Butler's theories, is a nec-essary precondition for antiessentialist feminist politics. Rather than signifying a breakdown in political organization, dissent frees feminist politics to express frag-mentary qualities of every political subject. The mechanics of dissent reflect the sub-ject of politics even as they define exemplary political organization.

Antiessentialist arguments about gender do not definitively occupy a position from within feminism. Their preoccupation with the category 'gender' most directly affects the scholarship of feminists within the academy. Gender also undergirds the political project of feminism. But the antiessentialist distrust of political organiza-tion—which Butler describes as "unity," and Donna Haraway reconstitutes as "unities"—leads antiessentialist arguments towards projections which could al-most be called antifeminism. These positions are not antifeminist because the content of these writings dismisses feminism or actively attempts to dismantle fem-inism. Instead, antiessentialism repudiates feminism as a construct of political or-ganization, since organization depends upon solidarity and unity. The collective characteristics of solidarity and vision that ground feminism are in opposition to the bugbear of antiessentialist arguments: unity, and by extension, totality.

Unity in politics includes building solidarity between actors, coordinating actions, producing and reproducing collective subjects with common political goals, and attempting to systematize and theorize chaotic relations of power in order to contest those power relations. Unity also demands a larger vision of social, po-litical, and economic change. Even the discursive construction of gender and the intervention in the process which defines woman create too tight a web of possi-ble meaning, too restricted a notion of political change for antiessentialist positions on feminism. Totality, in its most banal postfoundationalist interpretation, is essentialist, and in its most threatening interpretation, unavoidably coercive.[30] As feminism represents one form of politics, the construct, however changing, embodies more than a momentary project: to build political organization around the category woman and at times gender, to affect structural changes, and to coordinate politically identified subjects in common politics.

Haraway and Butler provide a more scrupulously visible argument against formal political organization within feminism. They argue against structured organization, but even this position endorses political forms such as shifting coalitions and fragmentary subject positions. Political identification is not absent from their theories, but is in a constant state of flux. In this sense, political organization does not refer to such nebulous concepts as community or collectivity, since Haraway and Spivak both give clear reasons in support of certain kinds of community within feminist politics. For Haraway, this political systemization of communities is the problem she labels "totalizing," not communities themselves. In this sense, Haraway's argument regarding feminist politics, like Butler's, is antiorganizational.

MEMORIES OF PERSONAL POLITICS

The debate between Jenny Bourne and Diana Fuss over identity politics outlines the logic of recent antiorganizational positions within feminism. They connect present problems of identity politics to a slogan that also animated antiorganizational debates early in the second wave women's movement.[31] The slogan "the personal is political" frames their considerable differences around identity politics and its organizational effects for feminism. The quality of Bourne's and Fuss's differences around a slogan from thirty years ago illustrates the theoretical and political debt of present feminist theory to early second wave feminism. They both argue that the slogan produced and/or supported trends in feminist organizational forms, though they disagree about what those forms were and how the slogan negatively affected feminist politics. Their starkly oppositional conclusions illustrate how early second wave debates over the scope, role, and form of organization, in this case around the consciousness-raising group, continue to animate present feminist theories about politics.

The differences between Bourne's and Fuss's assessments of identity politics, I suggest, are based upon how they interpret the role of consciousness-raising groups. Their often contradictory positions teeter between the poles of a debate from the late sixties and early seventies over whether the consciousness-raising group should be a means to radicalize women or a constitutive site for feminist politics.[32] Bourne views identity as a potential first step toward building political identification with a wider range of struggles against exploitation and oppression. Fuss questions the efficacy of any personalized political identification, since politics becomes something the subject inhabits rather than enacts. Bourne presumes the consciousness-raising group as a springboard for radical politics, while Fuss assumes its fixity as a vehicle for feminist organization. In their analyses of present feminist trends, they both agree that identity politics, as merely the subject's self-identification, involutes the scope of politics. Yet even here they differ in one important respect: where Fuss maintains the contingency of the subject (and political organization), Bourne heralds the contingency of struggle for political organization. To understand how they can draw such different conclusions, we must unearth earlier debates about antiorganizational versus contingent politics of the consciousness-raising group.

In "Homelands of the Mind: Jewish Feminism and Identity Politics" Bourne charges identity politics as a political form with atomizing and individualizing politics in general and feminism in particular. She writes that in the early second wave the "organic relationship we tried to forge between the personal and the political has been so degraded that now the only area of politics deemed to be legitimate *is* the personal."(her emphasis)[33] Bourne emphasizes *as a political process* how feminists implicated formerly separate spheres of "the personal" in "the political." Solely personalized politics, she argues, impoverishes this project. To the detriment of present feminism, solidarity across differences and agendas formed through political struggle, in Bourne's argument, are aspirations of the past.

Fuss differs from Bourne, though not in her mistrust of identity politics, but in the terms of her position on feminist organization. Fuss, like Bourne, argues against politics defined through a naturalized political identity. She writes that "the problem with attributing political significance to every personal action is that the political is soon voided of any meaning or specificity at all, and the personal is paradoxically de-personalized."[34] She writes about the blurring of distinctions between personal and political, where nothing is not political and all actions are politics. She suggests that the slogan's problem as it informs identity politics lies in its overapplication and a misunderstanding about its import. Both Bourne and Fuss agree that politics that reside in the body cannot sustain feminism. Yet Fuss still labels Bourne's position as politically naive, and her argument as convincing but overblown.[35]

Both Fuss and Bourne read the phrase the personal is political in its earlier context as strategic, but strategic for whom and for what ends? Spivak's reiteration of the dictionary definition reminds us of the origins of the term: *strategic* refers to a "trick designed to outwit or surprise the enemy."[36] Fuss mentions this strategic aspect of the slogan, to draw marginalized voices—what she calls "minority group concerns"—into the center stage of politics.[37] Bourne stresses that the phrase represents one attempt to attract apolitical women into a political movement. In addition, Bourne argues that the phrase invokes the battle to develop a more active political role for previously quiescent women.[38] Marlene Dixon corroborates Bourne's analysis in an article entitled "Public Ideology and the Class Composition of Women's Liberation (1966-1969)." Dixon states, "The politics of psychological oppression and the injustice of discrimination were aimed at altering the consciousness of women newly recruited to the movement in order to transform personal discontent into political militancy."[39] As consciousness-raising groups addressed the daily aspects of women's oppression, they provided a supportive place to politicize women's individual experiences. From a political understanding of experience, women could build connections to other struggles. These arguments supporting consciousness-raising groups suggested that by developing a systemic critique, women would draw a political link between injustices they experienced and the injustices against others along lines of race, class, sexuality, or nationality. In addition, women in small groups could develop the skills necessary to make personal grievances overtly political and become activists.

Fuss argues that the import of "the personal is political" lay in its adherents' aggressive fight for the political legitimacy of the women's movement. The trivialization of women's critiques of sexism in existing political groups demanded more than better behavior or more attention to problems of sexism. Instead, advocates of "the personal is political" argued in favor of radical alteration of what constituted valid politics.[40] While the content of activist women's arguments did not alter, the slogan pointedly exposed the negligible value that progressive activists accorded to relations marked primarily by gender. Strategically, this phrase defined a feminist politics that demanded a forum among other political struggles. Marge Piercy, writing at the end of the sixties, passionately attests to the import of this feminist attack against the more established progressive movements:

> I know no man can tell any woman how to measure her oppression and what methods are not politics in trying to get up off her knees. . . . We must have the strength of our anger to know what we know. No more arguments about shutting up for the greater good should make us ashamed of fighting for our freedom.[41]

If within the political category woman the slogan drew a larger and larger base of support for feminism, outside woman the slogan suggested a proposal to carve a terrain to exercise that growing political strength. Between experienced activists beginning to organize women, however, the political manifestations of the slogan "the personal is political" was hotly contested. The debate played out between the advocates of feminist antiorganization and proponents of political organization within feminism.

Antiorganizational theories of feminism in the sixties and early seventies operated within a vision still based on collective political activism. The subject of feminism was still interpellated through the demands of feminist organization. The personal became political through consciousness-raising groups, not through any intrinsically feminist act of will. If the women's movement succumbed to changing theories of what constitutes politics, whether defined through individualized changes in lifestyle or through consumption habits, consciousness-raising groups were also transformed from earlier incarnations. For this reason, I strongly disagree with Fuss's analysis that the downfall of defining the personal as political was due to a misunderstanding of the slogan.

Bourne ends her article with two arguments which open up a less reductive politics than the contingent subject of postfoundationalism. First, she posits that 'identity' cannot remain a static political category, but that feminists must constantly define and redefine what constitutes identity through political struggle. Second, she argues that the site of that redefinition of identity must take place in wider and wider circles of political solidarity. She quotes Franz Fanon in her plea to open up feminism to the struggles against exploitation and oppression:

> The mistake is to view identity as an end rather than a means. We do not need to seek out our identity for its own sake, but only to discover in the process "the universality inherent in the human condition," and, in that knowledge, commit ourselves to forming the correct alliances and fighting the right fights.[42]

Bourne's argument holds an additional commonality with Fuss's commitment to antiessentialism. Identity, as Bourne formulates a renewed category in this passage, is a means. While identity is strategic, it never loses the contingency of its meaning, even as a strategic concept. Bourne relates the process of identity to the process of politics and building political solidarity. The production of a political ideology, of the ability to "commit ourselves to forming the correct alliances," has none of the constant negotiation of meaning proposed by Butler. Bourne emphasizes the contingency of the conditions of struggle, not of the subjects engaged in struggle.

Fuss uses Bourne's definition of politics to provide the example of why Bourne's case is, in her words, "overstated." She responds that energizing the old slogan "the personal is political" does not require building greater political solidarity, as Bourne states, but demands a reading towards "reassessing and *repoliticizing*" politics based on naturalized identities (her emphasis).[43] Fuss concentrates on a misreading of the slogan. The failure of identity politics, Fuss argues, derives from a tragic collapse between personal and political. She asserts, "A severe reduction of the political to the personal leads to a telescoping of goals, a limiting of revolutionary activity to the project of self-discovery and personal transformation."[44] Further, she suggests that with a clearer understanding of what political identities mean, identity politics can be recharged as a political force. Unlike Bourne's, Fuss' remedies remain at the level of consciousness, of how politicized subjects understand (or misunderstand) their politics.

While Fuss and Bourne share similar elements in their critiques (and definitions) of identity politics, they draw opposite conclusions. Bourne argues that politics demands greater solidarity among feminists and within feminism. In contrast, Fuss concludes that a lack of broad ideological and political unity is not feminism's weakness. Fuss's dissatisfaction with Bourne's argument is clearer when compared to her definition of politics. For Fuss, even strategic essentialism is largely untenable since this position does not question the need for some political solidarity. Instead, Fuss "seeks to undermine the idea that politics must be steady and localizable, untroubled by psychic conflict or internal disorder."[45] The problem, argues Fuss, is not that feminism lacks solidarity, but that feminism holds onto problematic tenets of what can constitute feminist political organization. Identity politics, for Fuss, has an excessively rigidifying structure. To remedy this weakness, feminist dependence on organization itself must break down, and not just those forms of organization grounded in essentialist conceptions of women's biology or women's experience.

In response to Fuss's demand that we remember the history of the slogan, I take issue with her wholly textual reading of its contextual location within feminism. The definition of political, even derived through a limited notion of the personal, does not necessarily mean individualized goals for change. The organizational form which mobilizes the personal must also be taken into account. In the women's liberation movement, the consciousness-raising group mobilized women through experience and energized a slogan describing its politics.[46] This same organizational form allowed feminism to manage dissent through ideological fragmentation rather than confronting and prioritizing feminist political values.[47] The ensuing ideological fragmentation further dissipated solidarity built up between members and groups within and outside of the women's movement. In this sense, the consciousness-raising group, with its diffuse goals, strategies, and membership, worked in dialectical relation to competing definitions of personal politics. Decentralization defused political differences within feminism. Rather than creating a means to debate those differences, decentralization assisted the move away from collective politics, in Bourne's terms, "those bridges built between movements, groups, and activists." Commitments to a loose coordination, or even a future connection, between antiorganizational groups within the women's movement waned. As a result, I argue, the politicized subject (or identity) took center stage in feminist theories of politics.

EXPERIMENTS IN STRUCTURELESSNESS

Structurelessness, the term for early theories about antiorganizational feminist politics, was not the defining ideology of the consciousness-raising group. While its tenets gained legitimacy in the early seventies, structurelessness did not hold sway throughout the cities with numerous women's movement groups.[48] The terms of the debate over the role of the consciousness-raising group in women's liberation turned on several issues. One issue was the coordination of campaigns and political coherence in the movement. But another was the importance of politics, and the conscious, collective political subject in consciousness-raising groups and in the women's movement as a whole.[49] Consciousness-raising groups were meant to create wider support for women's liberation, but by the early seventies seemed to have failed in that goal.[50] Consciousness-raising groups, some charged, spent more time on their own needs rather than on furthering political struggle. In these critiques, consciousness-raising groups were not the movement, but one part of the movement. They were a means, not an end. The debate over consciousness-raising groups and personal politics hinged on the relationship of a collective subject to politics.

The ideological purpose of the personal in politics was one of dismantling the distinction between public and private relations. As the private experiences of women were aired publicly, the collective nature of these relations for all women would be revealed. But Shulamith Firestone locates another aspect—one that includes the quality of political means, and the ends produced through another form of organization. She writes that the combination of the personal with the political "is developing a new way of relating, a new political style, one that will eventually reconcile the personal—always the feminine prerogative—with the public, with the 'world outside,' to restore that world to its emotions, and literally to its senses."[51] Firestone credits the blurring of distinctions between what is public and private with the potential to develop new forms of social relations. This political style was an ideological ethos guiding the organization of the women's movement, and had internal effects for the women's movement as well.

In an organizational sense, putting the personal into politics increasingly signified abandoning the structures of organization. Within the self-defined women's movement, these principles were called "structurelessness," and were given the organizational form of consciousness-raising groups. Structurelessness worked well with the emotional and instinctual guidelines for radical feminist activism described by Firestone. Structurelessness and consciousness-raising were used within the largely white and northern student movements, such as SDS, in the early and mid-sixties, and the youth group of the civil rights movement, SNCC. Both movements were committed to participatory democracy.[52] Developed in the early sixties, theories of participatory democracy repudiated top-down hierarchies of the Left and had two central components. First, participatory democracy meant that progressive movements developed their policies with careful consideration of opinions from below, that is, from the organization's membership base. Second, it meant that the control over those decisions could not be concentrated in the hands of the leaders at the top. All members' opinions, quite literally, counted.[53]

Elinor Langer's essay entitled "Notes for the Next Time" charts the political activism of the sixties through its political-emotional effects on her thinking.[54] She marks a political closure not of formal organization in the sixties, since most student organizing in both the North and the South denounced hierarchical structures, but of organization as a site defining the collective subject. Langer writes hopefully about political fragmentation and the growth of personalized politics. Larger writes that there are "In one corner great numbers of decent people with a clearer understanding of the degeneration of American politics and a host of new energies and techniques with which they hope to escape degeneration or oppose it: diffuse and not always self-conscious personal liberation movements, communes, workers' resistance, consumer boycotts, cooperatives, alternative schools, religion."[55] She describes a more general impetus of political activism in the seventies, which also affected currents within feminism, away from collective politics. American politics had suffered a crisis of confidence in people's understanding. Therefore, they chose political fragmentation as one form to combat and avoid the stigma associated with collective politics.

Proponents of the diffusion of organizational skills hoped to undermine the corruption linked to politics. But, at least at first, "the personal is political" as a slogan for a women's movement did not work to disband collective consciousness. Instead, the slogan represented efforts to enlarge designations of political, or organization-based, activism. An early pamphlet, published in 1968 and known as the "Gainesville position," agitates in favor of an experiential and deeply personal politics of the women's movement.[56] Beverly Jones and Judith Brown, in "Toward a Female Liberation Movement," do not, however, renounce collective politics. They describe the importance of consciousness-raising for building solidarity between women: "We are a class, we are oppressed as a class, and we each respond within the limits allowed us as members of that oppressed class. . . . There is no personal escape, no personal salvation, no personal solution."[57] They argue that as women recognize their own conditions as part of the larger relations of sexism they will not turn inward, back to the purely personal, but toward political organization with other women. The answer to women's condition is not personal changes or growth. Instead, personal experiences provide the impetus for political (and collective) consciousness.

The same year that Jones and Brown published their pamphlet, Pam Allen first formalized the principles behind the consciousness-raising group as an organizational building block of the women's movement.[58] In Allen's widely read pamphlet, *Free Space*, the consciousness-raising group, because of its limited size, is said to operate without established channels for disagreements or formal structures to systematize goals and strategies. Likewise, the consciousness-raising group is not designed to function as a cohesive entity in political protest; therefore, it lacks the need for an elected leadership. Instead, the consciousness-raising group provides a forum for politically active women and apolitical women alike to discuss their ideas, activism, and feelings. According to Allen, "If the group is the place for women to develop their ideology, it would be most beneficial to the interaction within the group if the individual members were not all involved in the same political activity."[59] The consciousness-raising group, in Allen's description, functions as a site to reflect on and analyze women's political activism, not as the organizing tool for the women's liberation movement.

Yet only a year after Allen published *Free Space*, the consciousness-raising group became one central model for the political organization of women. As an organizational form, consciousness-raising groups retained the aspects Allen cites: localized concerns and decentralized political programs, as well as a lack of formal leadership roles and decision-making structures. In a memo from the early seventies, two years after Allen published *Free Space*, she wrote a constructive critique of the role of consciousness-raising in the women's liberation movement in which she clarifies the role of consciousness-raising groups in relation to structurelessness. Allen argues in her paper, "A Proposal for Women's Liberation to Develop Action Organizations," that consciousness-raising groups had led to unsustained political programs and campaigns, unaccountability among members to their consciousness-raising group and to the women's movement as a whole, and loss of the movement's short-term memory about what worked and did not work. She suggests forming an "action organization" as a next step toward building WLM activists out of the consciousness-raising groups. Allen illustrates a central component of the loose alliance between consciousness-raising groups, bridging dissent within the WLM:

> It is time that we began to coordinate our activities around a consistent analysis and program. The only way we will see if we are right (or who was right on what issue) is to free ourselves to explore our theories by finally putting them into practice. I, for example, do not believe in spontaneity of feelings as the basis for action, as I will explain later. Yet I do not wish to prevent other women who do believe in this type of political activity from following through on it. We belong to different organizations, however, for as long as we are together we will prevent each other from following our own consciences.[60]

Allen argues that the action organization could provide greater ideological cohesion within WLM, and literally put into practice the wide-ranging ideologies informing feminism. While the small group diffused some of the tensions between theories of feminism, it also led to the predominance of talk over action. Interestingly, around this same time, the Boston-area WLM experimented with a similar structural addendum to the consciousness-raising group. Meredith Tax, of the socialist group Bread and Roses, wrote about a similar formation functioning in 1969. She calls it a "project group," formed to combat the lack of long-term strategy and consistency in WLM politics.[61] Again, Tax emphasizes the importance of experimenting with organizing strategies and maintaining a collective memory about these different strategies for the whole movement to draw upon.

Even if defined by the organizational form of the consciousness-raising group, feminism encompassed a wide range of political activity and groups. In 1970 a reconstituted group, the New York Radical Feminists, published guidelines for what they called a "nuclear leaderless/structureless" collective.[62] Drawing from their stated history in the New York Radical Women, Feminists, and Redstockings, the Stanton-Anthony Brigade outlined its new organizational form in a manifesto entitled "Organizing Principles of the New York Radical Feminists." The manifesto espouses "a structure designed to promote the development of an organic group cohesion as opposed to a cohesion forced by external rules and regulations."[63] Structurelessness promotes an "organic" unity over an outside structure. This natural quality of unity among the members provides another basis for structure—one without the imposed, or "external," structures of human intervention. The project for the group, according to Alice Echols, was not primarily ideological change, but to reformulate how the women's movement functioned.[64] Women's movement groups, including some small groups, had experimented with highly structured organizational styles, with strict rules about participation and membership. The New York Radical Feminists' manifesto proposed a departure from internally divisive organizations. To this end their piece did not debate particular forms of organizing women, or specific aspects of these forms; instead, they located coercion in feminist organizing *within conscious structure itself.* By promoting a natural structure, New York Radical Feminists hoped to avoid mistakes of the past.

While the connections between participatory democracy and structurelessness include dispersed power within organizations, the terms of debate differed significantly in the women's liberation movement. Rather than target the means of organization, top-down leadership, unequal access to power by common members, and unfair systems to manage dissent, in debates about feminism, structure itself was held primarily responsible for the coercive effects of a collective movement. Early articulations of structurelessness within feminism expressly contradicted the more rigid organizational forms and the tightly controlled leadership positions that had developed in the late sixties within the student New Left movement.[65] Nevertheless, these positions linked this overtly antiorganizational critique through new organizational forms such as consciousness-raising groups.[66] Structurelessness, and the critique of political organization, often supported arguments for a personal politics. Structurelessness, however, was not the only position on women's movement structure that mobilized consciousness-raising groups.

Unlike the more extreme advocates of structurelessness, Jones and Brown remained committed to the creation of an organization. Alert to the failures of the student-based New Left, they tried to conceptualize a movement without its exclusionary hierarchy. As one basis for a separatist movement for women, they supported monthly meetings for politically active women in integrated movements. Rather than attempt to organize consciousness-raising groups into a movement, they propose that the consciousness-raising group draw together women from a variety of political commitments. They write, "I cannot make it too clear that I am not talking about group therapy or individual catharsis (We aren't sick, we are oppressed). I'm talking about movement. Let's get together to decide in groups of women how to get out of this bind, to discover and fight the techniques of domination in and out of the home.[67] In this sense, consciousness-raising groups could operate both within and without structured political organization. They would then bring together politically active women from a range of organizations, with nonactivist women to build solidarity across groups and movements. Together, women in consciousness-raising groups would produce a specifically political category, woman. The basis for women's political organization under the rubric woman begins from the small group as a support group, but develops into a site for political antiorganization. Jones and Brown prefigure Langer's hopeful description of decentralized, and even individualist, politics in the early seventies. Like Langer, they do not abandon the goal of structural change in their support for individual struggles.

Jones and Brown conflated organization around race and gender to argue for a separatist women's movement—separate in its political content and in its political form. They describe a movement defined by women fighting their own oppression, and state that "[w]omen mobilized where they stand against the nearest oppressor" will undermine the conditions of their oppression.[68] For Jones and Brown, to define oppression as one's own, or as relations experienced personally, produces first an individualized, then a collective, battle. When women are fighting "where they stand," the conflation between the personal and the political becomes less of a collective political identification with woman than an individual's confrontation as part of a larger movement. The subject of politics, in fighting from her own social and economic location, determines the basis for political solidarity. Participatory democracy sees leadership through the terms of the organization, as a means to promote democracy within the organizational structure. Consciousness-raising groups, for Jones and Brown, allow a dispersed politics of place, uncoordinated by a larger group. Participatory democracy, in their vision, is collective by default, because other women also face similar problems. While consciousness-raising groups may have collective elements, the politics, if not individualist, are highly localized by the natural unity of common experience.

The contradiction between feminist antiorganizational theories and the organizational forms that support these theories is not resolvable. Even in these early writings, antiorganizational theories about feminism envision loose coalitions on the basis of a subject status, woman. Whether a women's movement functions as a clearinghouse to discuss political activism or as a distinct movement, even structurelessness within feminism posits structures to enable the movement's goals. Jo Freeman, under her pseudonym "Joreen," attacks the tenets of antiorganizational consciousness-raising groups in "The Tyranny of Structurelessness." She cogently reviews the effects of informal small groups on a women's movement. As her title suggests, she argues that to reject organization leads to coercive relations within feminist politics.

As a response to women's exclusion in student politics, Freeman argues that the political organization of woman should not further weaken decision-making processes: structurelessness only mirrors the informality of women's exclusion in politics. She writes that:

> the idea [of a structureless group] becomes a smoke screen for the strong or the lucky to establish unquestioned hegemony over others. This hegemony can be so easily established because the idea of "structurelessness" does not prevent the formation of informal structures, only formal ones. . . . Thus structurelessness becomes a way of masking power. . . . As long as the structure of the group is informal, the rules of how decisions are made are known only to a few and awareness of power is curtailed to those who know the rules.[69]

For Freeman, power does not reside in the actual rules or policies of groups. Instead, she argues that structure provides a means for new members, or less powerful factions within groups, to access power over collective decisions. These structures provide recognized avenues to disagree with existing leadership and a forum to debate these differences. Rejecting structures within groups or movements, Freeman persuasively argues, cannot disband the power that inheres in these structures, but transforms and creates unrecognized and thereby invisible mechanisms of power. Freeman reiterates an important contradiction in antiorganizational theories about feminism, for even groups with no visible structures have structures. I would extend Freeman's thesis, to argue that even politics without visible theories of political change operate on the basis of assumed strategies. The erasure of subject and organization in politics only masks, but cannot fully dismantle, the theories at work.

Jo Freeman's article also expresses a widely voiced discontent with the lack of internal direction within the women's movement. By 1969, women active in feminist politics published articles criticizing localized small groups as too individualist, too divorced from any collective politics.[70] Structurelessness, Freeman argues, affects any attempts at coherence within the rubric "women's movement," since localized groups, even those within one city, so rarely coalesce towards common goals. Dissent between groups is managed through a greater and greater diffuseness concerning the question of what politics and what goals are feminist. Feminism, as an ever-expanding movement, avoids having to define its political tenets and direction. The absurd yet logical extension of the all-encompassing category feminism leads to the oft-mentioned question in feminist literature from the early seventies, "Is Jackie Onassis our ally?"[71]

Marked at its inception with wide differences over its political vision, the women's liberation movement, and even the more encompassing women's movement, could not claim any representative coherence. "Unity" as a call to rally feminism in the sixties and early seventies refers more accurately to attempts to create solidarity or broaden their base within localized groups rather than to any wider movement-based stratagem, imperialist or otherwise. Even in the late sixties, when Dixon claims "the mystique of sisterhood" was at its peak, the women's movement in present terms was an undeniably contingent category. 'The women's movement' denoted a political invention marked by very loose coalitions over any singular, structured organization. The ideological cohesion of an essentialist and homogenous category, woman, explains a host of ills in the feminism of the early seventies. The homogenous category woman did help sideline more complex articulations of feminism which included fighting racism, imperialism, and class-based elitism. The ideological diversity within the women's movement, however, was wide. The politics about and by women of color, immigrants, and lesbians were excluded because of the tyranny of the majority, not merely because of an essentialist analytic and political category, woman.

Some feminists, such as Meredith Tax and Pam Allen, argue that consciousness-raising groups should provide emotional support and a space for political analysis as one part of a larger political struggle. Others, such as Beverly Jones and Judith Brown, emphasize that consciousness-raising groups *are* the women's movement. In the latter position, the articulation of women's oppression itself constitutes feminist politics. Histories of the early second wave women's movement characterize consciousness-raising groups more generally. Consciousness-raising groups are either a decentralized organizational form that carries on the civil rights and student left vision of radical democracy, or the site for early articulations of feminist theory.[72] The former description is illustrated in a widely published 1970 position paper by the New York Radical Feminists. Their paper contends that consciousness-raising groups are an antihierarchical response to the rigidity of organizational forms in longer-term and geographically broad groups and political networks. Rather than trying to unite a fractious movement through regional and national meetings, consciousness-raising groups provide a solution to dissent within the women's movement's membership: increasingly amorphous boundaries of political organization. Early arguments in favor of decentralization (as a means to combat coercion or exclusion in feminism) continue to sustain and inform current arguments against the political organization of women.

ORGANIZATIONAL FORMS FOR PRESENT ANTIORGANIZATIONAL POLITICS

Despite shared analytic concerns, antiessentialist politics today are not organizationally in agreement with most marxist, postcolonial or antiracist politics. As proposals for redefining the politics of feminism, they stand for the dismantlement of organization rather than its transformation. Postfoundationalist suspicion of any formal political organization as totalizing, imperialist, and coercive creates a spontaneous conception of politics. Feminist politics of a contingent subject provides rich possibilities for antiracist arguments for nonreductive understandings of feminism and women.[73] The feminist politics of antiorganization, however, is antithetical to the struggle for greater and more complex feminist inclusion within political organization. As I argue in chapter 2, antiracist critiques of feminism, from those by Audre Lorde and Adrienne Rich to Deborah McDowell, attack organizational weaknesses in feminism that sustain and reproduce racism.[74] Even comments about the behavior and ideologies of particular feminists, in this approach, must be understood through the relationship of these members to feminism as an organizational constituency. The category most destabilized by the postfoundational analysis is feminism as a political formation. Antifoundationalist analyses question the boundaries which posit a stable or given category, feminism. But such theorists as Judith Butler and Donna Haraway condemn feminist political organization itself, not the ideological assumptions informing feminism nor the structures enabling feminism. Racism, elitism, homophobia, and hierarchy in these postfoundationalist analyses are inextricably part of any organizational structures of feminism, not in the relations of a feminist political praxis.

For postfoundationalist theorists, however, to denounce organization is not to avoid organizational forms altogether. Like the earlier antiorganizational theorists of feminism, they do propose particular organizational forms, such as Butler's coalitional assemblage or Haraway's affinity. Butler does not advocate the rejection of representational politics, but she challenges the limitation of feminism through essentialist categories such as woman. Any essentialist subject for feminism, no matter how strategic its definition, must be defined through exclusion, through what woman is not. Any category grounding feminism as a political or organizational formation can only do so through "coercive and regulatory consequences."[75] Instead, Butler proposes an alternative basis for an open-ended feminism, "one that will take the variable construction of identity as both a methodological and normative prerequisite, if not a political goal."[76] Butler harnesses Joan Scott's demand for a radical epistemology of woman and women to a feminist politics, one located within the structures, institutions, and relations that produce the subject.

Unlike earlier antiorganizational theories of feminism, the small group does not play any significant role in present formulations. The abdication of leadership does not further Butler's vision, but she does retain hope in fragmentary and far-flung coalitions. Neither does Butler propose to dismantle leadership hierarchies within feminism. Instead, she challenges even a momentarily fixed political solidarity: unity. In a series of leading questions, Butler links feminists' reliance on unity to continuing questions over what constitutes feminism and what that term includes and excludes. "Does unity," she asks rhetorically, "set up an exclusionary norm of solidarity?" "Unity" here becomes questionable in itself, rather than the particular forms or processes building unity. In order to skirt any political coercion based on arbitrary definitions of unity, Butler supports a coalitional politics of a constantly changing character. This antiessentialist form of feminist politics preempts neither "the shape nor the meaning of a coalitional assemblage" beforehand.[77] Instead, solidarity within politics dissolves and reconstitutes itself constantly, changing with the demands of institutions and structural axes of power. Pointedly, solidarity does not change due to any prefigured ideas of what should (or even could) occur. In this way, Butler substantiates her vision of feminist politics without determinism and without categorically enforced exclusion.

Butler provides one direction for antiorganizational theories of feminism. She even names a new organizational form, the coalitional assemblage. However, she does not demonstrate how this form would operate within feminism. An earlier quotation in this chapter by Donna Haraway describes coalitional assemblages, or affinity-based coalitions, between women making chips in Asia and women spiral dancing in a Santa Rita jail. Haraway sheds light on the organizational mechanism of this form. She describes women through her imagined affinity:

> The actual situation of women is their integration/exploitation into a world system of production/reproduction and communication called the informatics of domination. The home, workplace, market, public arena, the body itself—all can be dispersed and interfaced in nearly infinite, polymorphous ways . . . which make potent oppositional international movement difficult to imagine and essential for survival.[78]

Haraway, like Butler, rejects any natural basis for her affinity-based coalitions. Like Butler, and unlike early antiorganizational writers' descriptions of structure-lessness, she does not substitute the biological unity of women with an experiential solidarity between women.[79] Haraway formulates this potential coalition through factors of subject positionality within capitalism. The women in her example are defined through their relation to capitalism, through exploitative labor and the regulatory State. These women are indeed cyborgs, extant in her discussion not through individuality nor human agency, but as units constructed through the relations of global capital.

One aspect that remains unclear in Haraway's cyborg is whether the Santa Rita spiral dancer is a metaphor for a collective entity of similarly positioned structural locations (an antihumanist version of Jones and Brown's experiential unity), or whether it is a discrete unit on its own. Regardless, this singular/collective unity is interpellated through objective structures in itself/themselves as part of an affinity-based coalition, never for itself/themselves as part of a political organization or as a politically mobilized consciousness. True to her tenets of antiessentialist politics, Haraway's contingent, though certainly not random, units of affinity have no subjective dimension in their political organization.

Still, Haraway's theory of antiorganizational politics does not explain how women incarcerated in Santa Rita will construct this emancipatory coalition with Filipino workers, since this fragmentary unity is structured through the relations of political economy alone. Haraway's theory of feminist organization emerges from thin air. She does not, nor can she account for the production of an affinity-based coalition: when, how, or, indeed, why it may draw its strength. Unlike essentialist theories of the organic unity of consciousness-raising groups in the early seventies, Haraway's theory does not rely on the intrinsic will of people to organize, to fight for freedom, or to build solidarity. Haraway's spontaneous politics are antihumanist since she depends on the structural relations of capital to engender the very processes of political organization. Rather than theorize this struggle, Haraway falls into the theoretical vacuity of an antihumanist voluntarism.

In this sense, the problem posed to feminism by antiessentialist arguments is not primarily their deconstruction of the humanist subject for feminist politics, but their deconstruction of political organization in feminism. Because they reject organizational structures and relations, postfoundationalist positions cannot address either part of organization—theory or practice. That is, they cannot theorize the processes of politics, nor can they propose the means to build political solidarity. Postfoundationalist critiques of organization, which locate coercion in structure itself, lack any recognition of struggle. Without struggle, their only option is to fall back on a capitalism-driven and spontaneous conception of politics. Without a coherent articulation of these political processes, the antiessentialist support for dissent is meaningless. Coalitional assemblages and affinity-based coalitions, devoid of any enduring political and ideological positions, are much closer to a pluralist notion of an all inclusive, big-tent feminism. Dissent becomes the means to rationalize a feminism unanchored by any firm commitments to the character or content of their oppositional politics. The other possibility for antiessentialist politics is to revert to the tyranny Freeman discussed in 1970, of de facto power for the group or groups with the greatest cache/capital/power, who can then set the political agenda.

Pam Allen and Meredith Tax, in the late sixties and early seventies, suggest another means to negotiate dissent within feminism. They propose "action organizations" and "project groups" against the inclusive pluralism of the loose alliance between consciousness-raising groups. While retaining an ideological diversity, these action/project groups enact their theories of politics. Differences within feminism shift from the battle of words to their relative qualities in struggle. Allen and Tax frame their suggestions as a way to develop political knowledge within the women's movement. More importantly, they are both interested in the systematization of this knowledge to create a more cohesive and directed program for feminist politics. Both action organizations and project groups are vehicles, based in struggle, to promote greater unity of purpose, ideology, and action within feminism. While from different ideological positions in feminism, both Allen and Tax promote structure and organization in the women's movement.

Jenny Bourne discusses her alternative to identity politics with a similar commitment to organization and contingency in struggle. As one organizational form, identity politics—like consciousness-raising groups—is a means of furthering political identification. To reiterate a passage cited earlier:

> The mistake is to view identity as an end rather than a means. We do not need to seek out our identity for its own sake, but only to discover in the process "the universality inherent in the human condition," and, in that knowledge, commit ourselves to forming the correct alliances and fighting the right fights.[80]

Identity politics can strengthen political identifications between groups and struggles for what she calls "the right fights." She does not promote political struggle to prove a theory correct or misguided, but to shift the terms of identity politics from the subject in politics to political struggle. She does, however, see identity politics as a means to discover what those "correct alliances" and "right fights" are. Her adjectives—*correct* and *right*—do not promote a relativism between struggles so much as a belief that some fights and alliances are correct, while others are not. Bourne's appeal, through Fanon, to "universality inherent in the human condition" is also directed towards building an informed and conscious unity, not deconstructing it.

In Bourne's analysis, dissent, whether internal or external to the women's movement, is part of the same dialectical process. Struggle operates on the terrain of political organization and political struggle. For example, the practice of struggle is imbricated in the demands both of building solidarity within a political organization, and of furthering an explicit political program. Struggle also has a dialectical character. The practice of struggle produces changes in the conditions for political organization as its specific character is transformed by those conditions. Struggle, as an act, marks the processes of political struggle, including how those processes create and recreate identities. "Identity," says Bourne, "is not merely a precursor to action, it is also created through action."[81] In Bourne's analysis, struggle does not encompass the entire range of social, economic, and political forces at work in the production of identities. The contingency of struggle affects these factors of political organization, not only, as in postfoundationalism, the subject producing and produced through struggle.

FOUR

LESBIAN SEXUALITY BECOMES
AN ISSUE

The first three chapters of this book illustrate how theory intersects with politics in feminism. Chapter 1 posits the importance of organization to the early second wave feminist movement and to how we continue to conceive of feminism. Chapters 2 and 3 show the second wave lineages of two enduring and problematic feminist precepts: first, that pluralism can advance feminist goals, and second, that antistructure in feminist groups can eliminate hierarchical relations between members. In these chapters, I outline the politics engendered by theory and discuss how our assumptions delimit our political horizons. Chapter 2 shows how pluralism frames feminist racism as exclusion and suggests inclusion as an antiracist goal. Chapter 3 argues that postfoundationalist support for indeterminacy, like the earlier experiments with group structurelessness, dismantles any organizational accountability to its membership and its politics.

Both chapters 2 and 3 center on how dissent functions within the perimeters of the women's movement, even as the debates' participants exceeded those self-identified boundaries.[1] Dissent, as a site of feminist struggle, focuses inward and ignores how centrally internal and external struggles affected each other. Neither of these chapters asks how these issues, racism in chapter 2 and structurelessness in chapter 3, emerged and developed as issues alongside, within, and sometimes against feminism. Instead, the issues occupy a center stage in debates about feminism as if by historical necessity rather than by conscious decisions or in response to a range of socioeconomic and political forces. Each issue carries a complicated theoretical and political story—a story often told as history. This chapter draws on those histories of sexuality and lesbians in the women's movement to understand how lesbian sexuality as an issue created particular imperatives for the U.S. women's movement in the late sixties and early seventies. As Gary Lehring powerfully illustrates, the goals articulated by the gay liberation movement in the late sixties also carry theoretical and political lessons for activists today.[2] This chapter's memory-work concerns an issue's function in the gay and women's liberation movements rather than its trajectory into the present. Both projects about the history of an issue and the issue's mechanics within organization, however, attempt to theorize the political through the movements' own terms.

Lesbian sexuality as an issue was not simply absorbed into the women's movement after a successful fight against feminist homophobia. As an issue, lesbian sexuality forced changes in feminist ideology, goals, and conceptions of movement alliances and coalitions, even in how to define women's movement. As an issue, it was transformed from a lifestyle choice and subculture to a campaign goal and wider vision for social change. In particular, the issue of lesbian sexuality illustrates how fraught the transition is from single-issue alliances between movements to more intersectional coalitions based on common ideological commitments. Through a discussion about lesbian sexuality and the women's movement this chapter suggests that not only are political issues constructed, but issues construct movements. In this chapter and the following chapter I return to Rosa Luxemburg's formulation from chapter 1, positing the integral, mutually sustaining, and noncontiguous relationship between struggle and organization.

Martha Shelley, past president of the New York Daughters of Bilitis and a member of both the gay and women's liberation movements, frames the furor to admit lesbianism into feminism from another perspective. In her 1970 article "Lesbianism and Women's Liberation," Shelley writes about an American tradition of leniency towards lesbians, who were viewed as less threatening to heterosexuality than gay men. Before lesbian sexuality was linked to the feminist movement, she argues, it could be absorbed into heterosexuality as a fetish or illicit site of desire. After lesbian sexuality was implicated in women's liberation *as a movement,* its dubious status as nonthreatening was reversed. She avers, "[T]hey don't take women seriously enough to consider lesbianism a real threat—or didn't until the Women's Liberation Movement came along."[3] Shelley predicts in her essay that lesbians would face more danger of violent repression after this alliance. As more than a sexual desire and range of practices, lesbian sexuality was a site of often unorganized struggle. But as it became an organized site of struggle and a part of feminist goals for widespread social change, Shelly accurately predicted its more freighted connotations. Lesbian sexuality became as dangerous to heterosexual privilege as male homosexuality, if not more so.

Shelley astutely emphasizes that the women's liberation movement—when it began to organize around lesbian sexuality as an issue—changed its social context and thereby the very meaning of 'lesbian' as an issue in that context.[4] Lesbian sexuality, she argues, is never solely an issue or a set of social, economic, and political meanings in the abstract, but is embedded in constantly changing relations. Part of the meaning of lesbian in the late sixties and early seventies grew from its link, albeit contestatory, to the women's movement. If lesbian necessarily carried additional weight due to its relationship to the women's movement, the movement tried to manage and vocalize lesbian sexuality in more disparate ways—with varying degrees of containment. As lesbian was transformed through its relationship to the women's movement, throughout the women's movement, the politics of lesbian sexuality created paradigmatic shifts in analyses and politics.[5] The issue of sexuality could not be summed up with a simply framed demand for choice or control of one's own body, but began to challenge unstated heteronormativity within feminist goals.[6] The women's movement needed to be configured with more porous boundaries due to members' multiple organizational affiliations. Neither lesbian as a previously autonomous site of struggle nor the women's movement as a site of political organization wholly determined the relationship between them. In the last chapter, I will return to this dialectical relationship between struggle and organization with more precision.

Lesbian sexuality was not a unified issue even in its political forms, let alone in its targets, strategies, or goals. In this chapter, I discuss three general sites of struggle from 1969 to 1971, though lesbian sexuality as an issue developed in these struggles did not always operate discretely or contiguously. First, institutionalized homophobia dogged the women's movement and the fight against feminist homophobia was one issue vital to the movement's survival. Purging lesbian members or more subtle silencing, policing, and marginalizing of lesbians within women's movement groups was widespread.[7] Homophobia, not lesbians, divided feminist groups. Second, campaigns that targeted institutional and legal discrimination against lesbians and gays created alliances between different groups and movements.[8] These campaigns tended to supercede one group or movement's boundaries as wider circles of activists took political responsibility for an issue. At times, several of these issues, such as lesbian and gay civil rights campaigns, worked together. The goals were often clearly defined and seen as one step towards greater equality and justice. Third, analyses and campaigns that challenged heterosexist norms and privileges cohered around lesbian-feminist criticisms of sex roles and the nuclear family.[9] Through a systemic analysis of how heterosexuality structures our expectations, and more importantly, how it truncates our visions for transformative social change, lesbian sexuality created alternative possibilities for feminist organizing. These critiques constituted different conditions and frameworks for political activity rather than recognizably "lesbian issues." As a result, in this third form, lesbian sexuality often unsettled assumptions about discrete movement boundaries and disrupted attempts to build unfragmented and noncontradictory politics. In the last part of this chapter, I discuss how two feminist groups, Seattle Radical Women and Boston's Bread and Roses, framed their questions and positions on lesbian sexuality before and after 1969. These writings, whether manifestoes or issue-based papers, provide important insights about collective expressions of groups' self-representation and their changing political understandings. As collective documents, their discussions about lesbian sexuality in movement politics, in particular, help to reveal more generally how an issue is absorbed and mobilized around, and how it transforms a movement.[10]

FROM "OUR BODIES" TO "OUR MOVEMENT"

One central article, "Woman-Identified Woman," challenged feminists to rethink lesbian sexuality and lesbians in the women's movement.[11] The article was published after a highly visible zap action (a public spectacle designed to raise consciousness about an issue) at the 1970 Congress to Unite Women. The congress convened a wide range of women's groups, radical and liberal, to discuss feminist issues, campaigns, and strategies. A group of women, many active in both gay liberation and women's liberation movements, wearing T-shirts that read "lavender menace," took over the microphone at the congress and fielded a discussion about lesbians in the women's movement. The organizers of the action, many of whom later formed Radicalesbians, changed the terms for debates about homophobia and politics already raging in the women's movement. This action and many others raised questions about how to organize around goals that spanned different movements without losing organizational integrity, how to build an informed solidarity between movements, and how to allow for flexibility among movements.

The reasons why lesbian politics and the gay liberation movement grew so quickly and so forcefully in the late sixties and early seventies have been explored in richly suggestive scholarship. The works by Verta Taylor and Nancy Whittier, Alice Echols, Lisa Duggan, John D'Emilio, Barry D. Adam, and Martin Duberman, and recent autobiographies by Karla Jay and Susan Brownmiller, provide valuable information about the development of the gay liberation movement and groups such as Radicalesbians in this period.[12] They build on such early collections as Karla Jay and Allen Young's *Out of the Closets: Voices of Gay Liberation* and Donn Teal's overview *The Gay Militants* to show how lesbian sexuality as an issue changed feminist thinking and politics around sexuality, the family, the pro-woman position, and heterosexism.[13] Detailing how these politics became goals, campaigns, and sites of coalitional unity, they explore contradictions, strengths and weaknesses in these struggles. Their painstaking work of historical recovery, analysis, and commentary in many ways makes this chapter possible. Their historical preservation of how activists and groups enacted the radical politics of gay and lesbian sexuality inform my analysis of how an issue is configured and reconfigured in the process of political struggle.

Anne Koedt's touchstone article, "The Myth of the Vaginal Orgasm," confirms that the issue of women's sexuality fell solidly within early definitions of feminist politics.[14] Her article even suggests that bisexuality and lesbian sexuality were likely expressions of feminist women's sexual awakening. She argues that women's sexual pleasure, centered on clitoral instead of vaginal orgasms, destabilizes the inevitability of heterosexual sex. Koedt writes, "[I]t forces us to discard many 'physical' arguments explaining why women go to bed with men. What is left, it seems to me, are primarily psychological reasons why women select men at the exclusion of women as sexual partners."[15] Koedt endorses lesbian sexuality as one option for sexually aware women, not as the answer for sexually dissatisfied women. Nor does she discuss lesbian sexuality as a choice already made by many women, one that meant discrimination and violence against them due to the social demand for compulsory heterosexuality. In this quotation, lesbian sexuality—or perhaps more accurately, bisexuality—simply widens women's sexual possibilities. Even the welcome extended to lesbian sexuality by Koedt's article did not ensure its standing as an issue for the women's movement. In fact, lesbian sexuality did not enjoy immediate recognition as a feminist issue by any quarter of the second wave women's movement. Lesbian sexuality became an issue for feminism between 1969 and 1971, and as a result changed what feminism designates.

Betty Friedan made the derision of lesbian sexuality in the women's movement impossible to ignore. Friedan in 1969 and 1970 began to purge NOW membership of lesbians and actively fought to squelch discussions about lesbian sexuality in the group. Some members, such as Rita Mae Brown, actively opposed Friedan's policy; Brown wrote a memo about NOW's homophobia against its own membership. In a meeting about the memo, Friedan complained that lesbians were a lavender menace and would divide the movement. This phrase gained infamy and biting political responses as it concisely articulated an often unspoken assumption in mainstream lobbying groups like NOW as well as the more radical, countercultural women's liberation groups.[16] While not as openly hostile toward lesbians, women's liberation groups more often ignored lesbian sexuality within their membership and as a political issue. They supported women's sexual freedom from exploitative and oppressive relationships with men, but did not propose a lesbian sexuality alternative to heterosexuality. Some groups (such as Cell 16 and the Feminists) advocated celibacy, a formulation that tactically foreclosed sex as a feminist issue.[17]

Karla Jay, a member of the Gay Liberation Front (GLF) and the Feminists in New York City, writes in her memoir about the profound anger lesbians in the women's movement felt when Susan Brownmiller trivialized lesbian sexuality in her *New York Times* article about the women's liberation movement.[18] Brownmiller joked that lesbians were not the menace Friedan imagined, but merely a "lavender herring," a smear, like the taint of communism, lobbed against the women's movement.[19] Defined by intramovement labels like "menace" and "herring," lesbian sexuality was poised to be an issue first *within* the women's movement. Writing off lesbian sexuality as a fear tactic propagated by antifeminists may also explain why the issue of lesbian sexuality was largely absent from women's liberation manifestoes and political programs before 1970. The fear tactic worked.

Radicalesbians' essay "Woman-Identified Woman" attempted to explain the complaints of feminist lesbians to the women's liberation movement. Movement participants and historians have noted the accommodations the document makes to soften prejudices within the women's movement against open lesbians in the movement and lesbian sexuality as an issue.[20] "Woman-Identified Woman," in its very title, defines lesbian sexuality more through political affiliations than sexual desire, and seems to go along the grain of such groups as Redstockings and New York Radical Feminists that advocated a "pro-woman" line. As the Redstockings' Manifesto outlines the pro-woman position, "In fighting for our liberation we will always take the side of women against their oppressors. We will not ask what is 'revolutionary' or 'reformist,' only what is good for women."[21] The identification with women, rather than abstract ideologies, propels pro-woman politics. Lesbian sexuality, as described by the paper's title, was the expression of pro-woman politics.

But the document also pushes the logic of pro-woman to fight the trap of lesbian sexuality becoming an add-on issue and lesbians operating as a special interest group. They present pro-woman ideas with a more encompassing twist:

> Our energies must flow toward our sisters, not backwards towards our oppressors. As long as women's liberation tries to free women without facing the basic heterosexual structure that binds us in on-to-one relationship with our oppressors, tremendous energies will continue to flow into trying to straighten up each particular relationship with a man. . . . It is the primacy of women relating to women, of women creating a new consciousness of and with each other which is at the heart of women's liberation."[22]

Their argument effectively centers lesbian sexuality (or woman-identification) within feminism. It challenges the view of lesbian sexuality as a scare tactic by revaluing that taunt. It defines lesbian sexuality as the basis for women's solidarity; in fact, the point of unity rather than division. It criticizes with astonishing delicacy the centrality—to the consciousness-raising discussions so vital to the women's liberation movement in this period—of heterosexual relationships and seeing "men as the enemy." Lesbian sexuality is much more than one issue in "Woman-Identified Woman"; it is an ethos, an identity, a culture, and a politics. Lesbians are not a special interest group. They are the entire committed membership of the women's movement.

Lesbian sexuality infuses so much of the women's movement in this position paper it almost ceases to be an issue as such. In this vein, they imagine a liberated future when behavior and desire are not linked to sexual categories, a future where lesbian sexuality could not be an issue. Yet this paper does not erase extant distinctions between the gay liberation movement and the women's movement. They argue that gendered roles based on heterosexuality hurt women and men: "[L]esbianism, like male homosexuality, is a category of behavior possible only in a sexist society characterized by rigid sex roles and defined by male supremacy. . . . Homosexuality is a by-product of a particular way of setting up roles (or approved patterns of behavior) on the basis of sex. . . ."[23] In this passage, Radicalesbians introduces a wider category, 'sex', one that embraces more than biological gender difference. Sex includes desire and practices, the acts of sex. Since women and men enact their gender through sex, this analysis demands more complicated politics for feminists and gay activists alike.

In the Gay Liberation Front, women and men share the fight to dismantle these sex roles and dismantle the basis for homophobia, but lesbians and gays do not share every battle. Radicalesbians assert, with Martha Shelley, that lesbian sexuality functions differently than male homosexuality in society. They separate sexism and homophobia as they affect lesbians and gay men. Perhaps their clearest distinction between gay liberation and women's movements lies in the role of lesbian activists as instigators of changes within both of these movements. Gay men must fight their sexism and straight feminists must fight their homophobia. Their argument shows how lesbians can play central, even leading, roles in both of these struggles and, by extension, in both of these movements.

The statement by Radicalesbians outlines a definition of leadership within the women's movement that is potentially essentialist. Lesbians carry special status as leaders because of the very position they attack. To be a lesbian is a matter of sex roles and acts; to gain validity as a leader is to embody these characteristics. Depending on whether desire is seen as biological or social, a lesbian, and hence a feminist leader, can be either born or created. Lesbian sexuality, in "Woman-Identified Woman," can act within the women's movement as a verification of revolutionary credentials and a badge of leadership. Lesbian sexuality, in Radicalesbians' opening salvo, acts as a feminist issue primarily *within* the women's movement.

Alice Echols, in her history of radical feminism, locates the divisiveness of lesbian politics within feminism during the early seventies. She blames both straight feminists' resistance to lesbians and lesbian sexuality, and lesbian feminists' "dogmatism."[24] The combination of lesbians as the ultimate pro-woman feminists with the almost vanguard character attached to lesbian activists in the women's movement exacerbated a tendency towards holistic politics. In this model, it is not enough to fight to change relations or to struggle within those relations: politically pure activists must live the solution to those problems.[25] Choosing to individually enact political resolutions to movement struggles gained currency within the larger collective movement as well. Even the alliance between the Gay Liberation Front and the women's liberation movement was embodied by the activists who were members of both movements. An alliance through common members potentially atrophies both movements, since it attenuates movement-based links built of compromise, discussion, and understanding. Instead of developing as a movement or group in relation to each other, the connection depends on a much less reliable, albeit convenient, source. As an issue within the women's movement, lesbian sexuality does not have to be divisive; it can function as a site for unity, as Radicalesbians hoped. It was figured in ways, however, that made divisions almost impossible to avoid.

The GLF's women's caucus raise the fight against intramovement homophobia as one of common interests among feminist activists and, consequently, potential cross-movement coalitions. They state their third goal as one addressing oppressive sex roles in solidarity with the women's liberation movement:

> 3) Raising the consciousness of our sisters active in Women's Liberation to openly acknowledge and actively support lesbians, with the attitude of solidarity and not reciprocity. . . . We feel that the core oppression of women is the lesbian's oppression and the ultimate liberation of women is through the liberation of lesbians. Real freedom for lesbians will mean the end of all oppressive relationships based on male dominance and the compulsion women feel to seek male approval and support.[26]

Their description portrays homophobia as a struggle internal to feminism's fight against sexism, a position figured by a more contemporary term which denotes a specific sexism, *heterosexism*. The demand for "solidarity and not reciprocity" also portrays lesbian sexuality as an issue within feminism, not just a site for feminist support of Gay Liberation Front struggles. They also describe the struggle as one of overlapping movement interests, since the fight against homophobia ultimately betters the conditions for all women, heterosexual and lesbian. It does not challenge a specialized oppression for a particular subset of women, but the gendered relations in which all women (and men) participate. Lesbian sexuality is a feminist issue, but one that feminists should fight out of collective self-interest, not in sympathy for some women's plight.

At the 1971 NOW convention, members passed a resolution endorsing the rights of lesbians within the larger group and recognizing lesbian sexuality as a feminist issue. The resolution from the NOW convention solidly refutes its past policies and recognizes lesbian sexuality as an issue within the women's movement and as a feminist political issue:

> Be it resolved that N.O.W. recognizes the double oppression
> of lesbians.
> Be it resolved that a woman's right to her own person includes
> the right to define and express her own sexuality and
> choose her own lifestyle.
> Be it resolved that N.O.W. acknowledges the oppression
> of lesbians as a legitimate concern of feminism.[29]

By 1973, NOW began to provide intraorganizational support for the 1971 convention resolutions about lesbian sexuality when it formed the NOW Task Force on Sexuality and Lesbianism, headed by Sidney Abbott and H. Jayne Vogan.[27] In their first newsletter they advocated activities and asked questions for local NOW chapters to help them assess what issues could be raised in their area. The questionnaire asks whether chapters hosted local panels and discussions on sexuality and lesbian sexuality in particular, and about the availability of sex education programs and the character of municipal and state sex laws. The newsletter also asks members to measure their chapter's attitude towards lesbian sexuality. It describes three possible attitudes: "Liberal—a woman can feel comfortable as an open lesbian in the chapter, tolerant—lesbianism is all right but not a topic for discussion: what you do in bed is your own business, conservative—lesbianism is an illness."[28] The first option questions the group's attitude towards its lesbian members and whether NOW welcomes activists who define themselves as lesbians. By extension, this choice attempts to measure whether lesbian activists can work both within NOW and a gay rights group. The second option asks whether lesbian sexuality is allowed to be a feminist issue. If viewed as solely a bedroom issue, a series of acts or desires, or defined as private, then a "tolerant" NOW chapter cannot organize around lesbian sexuality or homophobia. The third option gets at the chapter's ideological character; lesbian sexuality in this choice is an issue, but not a feminist one. Presumably lesbians are not welcome if the chapter is conservative, unless they successfully hide their sexuality.

The task force newsletter pushes local chapters to consider what the 1971 convention resolutions meant within local groups. The questionnaire stays very close to the intention and scope of lesbian sexuality within these resolutions and views it as an issue internal to chapters' smooth functioning. It coopts the more far-reaching assertions by the Radicalesbians about leadership and movement alliances since the issue, in this early document, centers on how to create a more comfortable political environment for lesbians in NOW. But the newsletter also shows that the resolutions of two years before would not easily disappear from NOW's agenda and would not be ignored by the national organizational structure.

Heterosexism within the women's movement not only hurt unity among members, but damaged the struggles to free women of sexist expectations. This understanding could build feminist politics that operated outside of the confines of the movement. In 1973, when Betty Friedan published an article that attacked lesbians in the women's movement, representatives from the Lesbian Liberation Committee, Gay Activists Alliance, NOW, and New York Radical Feminists, and the American Civil Liberties Union, among others, convened an immediate joint press conference to condemn her comments. The names of the groups involved show that as an issue, homophobia could be a site for some kinds of coalitions. Even when activists worked on lesbian issues within women's liberation groups, gay liberation groups, or from a separatist formation, other possibilities existed for these groups and movements to coalesce. Leadership in a press conference is hard to assess and perhaps a simple, outraged reaction is the easiest moment for unity.

The concerted effort by women in a wide range of feminist groups to admit lesbian sexuality into feminism produced stunning changes. But even NOW's reversal did not assure the future security of lesbian sexuality as a feminist issue. An early historian and movement participant, Jo Freeman reports that after these resolutions passed, "[M]any N.O.W members still felt that lesbianism was not a feminist issue."[30] Her observation suggests important questions that cannot be fully explored by historical accounts. Activists' dedicated work in NOW and other women's liberation groups to raise the issue of lesbian sexuality does not fully illuminate how it functioned as an issue, particularly in its more theoretical state as an issue-based commitment. Likewise, a blow-by-blow account cannot uncover how a political issue implicates theory or the mechanics of the relationship between a political organization, in this case the amorphous women's movement, and a site of political struggle, in this case lesbian sexuality. This issue, like many, implicates more than one movement and can help to elaborate how movements operate in relation to (and distinct from) each other, even when those movements are as committed to decentralized alliances between internal groups as the early second wave women's movement and the emerging gay liberation movement. Lesbian sexuality as an issue brought the movements closer together to share the struggle against homophobia, but also heightened tension around questions of separatism and leadership for both movements.

NOW's resolution in 1971 evokes some of the gaps between feminist ideals and gay liberation politics through its attempts to bridge them. The first part of the resolution, about lesbians' double oppression, recognizes lesbians as one feminist constituency that faces particular conditions of oppression. In wording that prefigures the term *heterosexism,* the document attests to the differentiated analysis of woman that lesbian sexuality demands. But this differentiation is not purely analytic, since the resolution also asserts the ethical imperative for the women's movement to recognize lesbians by their sexuality, since the homophobia they face as lesbians compounds the sexism they face as women.

The second resolution from NOW's 1971 convention amends an accepted feminist issue: women's control over their bodies. They add two aspects to their program that already supported women's right to not marry, and to have full control over their reproductive life, including their right to a legal abortion. In this addition, women's sexual desires are also theirs to control and express. Their right to stay unmarried, by 1971, includes the right to have women as sexual partners. They frame sexual self-determination as a right that should have legal standing.

One additional resolution from NOW's convention in 1971 begins to articulate lesbian sexuality as more than just another issue of a vocal fragment. NOW supported the "child custody rights of mothers who are also lesbians."[31] NOW, characteristically, framed its challenge to the nuclear family as one of legal rights; but it represents a lesbian issue that groups throughout the women's movement grappled with: the feminist critique of the family. In the case of NOW, leadership by lesbians is contained within the issue of child custody, primarily a leadership of lesbians' special interests in changing this law. The demand does not attack the nuclear family outright, but chips away at the privileges enjoyed by the heterosexual parental unit. To a certain extent a legal change in lesbians' parental rights does redefine the family, but not necessarily the nuclear family. Lesbian sexuality still functions as one issue within NOW's larger agenda, an issue not noticeably integral to their ideology. Lesbian sexuality is an issue because women are lesbians. They fight homophobia in the law, but not heterosexist definitions of sex or sex roles.

Even in its critique of the heterosexual family, NOW mobilized around lesbian sexuality as a single issue.[32] As a single issue, lesbian sexuality drew in greater numbers of members and more fully represented existing members' interests. It fueled ongoing campaigns, particularly the formation of child care facilities and women's right to control their bodies. Perhaps most importantly, lesbian sexuality added urgency to ongoing radical ideological positions, such as the critique of women's oppression in the family. In this last sense, it revealed the heterosexist assumptions present in many accepted critiques of patriarchy and alternatives. The debate surrounding lesbian sexuality carved out new political terrain in the development of the critique of the family. As an ideological attack on marriage, heteronormativity, and the nuclear family, lesbian sexuality prefigured, in its very terms, a coalition-based strategy rather than one of an alliance based on a common single issue.

Framed as a critique of the family, lesbian sexuality was not a single issue because it produced an ideological shift in how the women's movement saw its present campaigns as well as its future goals.[33] This structural analysis of heterosexism demanded a more diffuse and far-reaching conceptualization of lesbian sexuality as an issue, one that touched many feminist campaigns and feminist ideas for change. The move toward coalitions, however, did not inhere in all strategies for lesbian sexuality as a site for feminist critique. Two positions vied for attention. The first proposed stronger coalitions between the Gay Liberation and the women's liberation movements based on common ideological commitments. The second argued that even coalitions were effectively impossible unless lesbian feminists had de facto leadership over those coalitions.[34] This second argument often functioned as one precursor to lesbian feminist separatism.

Joan Comedy, a member of the Washington, D.C., Gay Liberation Front, gave a speech at the August 26, 1970, Women's Rally, itself a demonstration of solidarity between movements. She aptly depicts how lesbian liberation activists refined the feminist critique of the family, declaring that lesbian sexuality "allows us to examine and to reject the whole nuclear family structure, which locks women to men and children to both, in a box that limits human growth and perpetuates the authoritarian, male dominated model of human relationships."[35] The nuclear family, gendered behavioral roles, and gendered sex roles all come under attack. Comedy describes a common lesbian feminist position that heterosexual relationships in the patriarchal family cannot be reformed. Capitalism overdetermines the oppressive quality of these relationships, and even the concerted effort by women and men cannot prevail in these conditions. Implicitly, Comedy criticizes feminist attempts to rehabilitate the nuclear family as a limited goal that reflects their heterosexual bias. She does not attack feminists' homophobic behavior or attitudes, but embeds her critique of heterosexism programatically and analytically in an accepted feminist issue. Lesbian sexuality, as a frame of reference, produced a critique of heterosexism in the family which otherwise did not exist anywhere in the early second wave women's movement.

The lesbian feminist critique of the family moved lesbian sexuality away from being an add-on issue within the women's movement toward being intrinsic to feminist theory and practice, that is, into feminist organization. Also in Washington, D.C., a statement by women who would later form a lesbian feminist group called the Furies, denounces heterosexist practices in the day-care center. They, however, produce different demands (than Comedy does) of the Gay Liberation Front for any coalition work on this issue. They describe their challenge as a structural, and not a solely issue-based, critique. "We are not just another special interest group asking for tolerance and a little part of the daycare center's program. As lesbians we are challenging the basic structure and value of the daycare center."[36] They urged other women and men in the collective to join their struggle, but on their terms.

The Furies and Gay Liberation Front activists such as Comedy produced an analysis of lesbian sexuality that guided feminist politics and theory. They propose the ambitious goal of dismantling the nuclear family. This campaign to end heterosexism in the family was one part of the larger struggle against sexism and, in Comedy's case, racism and capitalism. Neither document suggests that leadership inheres in lesbian activists because of their behavior or due to an innate sexual desire. But both, to different degrees, demand an ideological leadership in the feminist movement (and potentially in the gay liberation movement), a leadership defined by lesbian sexuality as a frame of analysis.

The fight over day care was an opening salvo by the Furies, but their mimeographed position paper reveals the importance of leadership to lesbian sexuality as a systemic feminist issue. Lesbian sexuality, they argue, should provide the ideological leadership of the women's movement. Unlike Radicalesbians' argument in "Woman-Identified Woman," they do not center lesbians at the forefront of feminist (and gay liberation) politics, though these two positions can certainly be linked. While the Radicalesbians' paper suggests the importance of specific people as leaders, the Furies' paper advances lesbianism's theoretical, and thereby strategic, primacy within feminism. Lesbian sexuality, in this second argument, is no longer a single issue nor an enlightened lifestyle/political choice. The Furies sought to force lesbian feminist positions to the forefront of gay liberation coalitions with women's liberation. As the self-appointed vanguard of both movements, lesbian feminist groups, like the Furies, were poised for a break from each movement, rather than operating as a bridge between them.

The Furies based its separatism on the political purity of an ideological leadership based on lesbian issues. Their group formed around a kind of ideological lesbian separatism. In contrast, Radicalesbians describes the process of lesbians leaving the Gay Liberation Front alongside the women's liberation movement as one of "coalescing."[37] The article does not shun either movement, but does not assert a special identification of Radicalesbians to either one. "Some sisters feel themselves to be an arm of the Woman's Liberation Movement. . . . Others feel themselves to be in close affiliation with GLF."[38] Both views existed within the one group. The possibility for separatism from both movements was strong. As one position paper suggests, lesbian feminists drew from "Woman-Identified Woman" and the Lavender Menace zap action the means to build a separate movement. As the paper "Notes on Dyke Separatism" states, the women's movement is as frustrating, if on different fronts, as the gay liberation movement.[39] The author(s) writes:

> Lesbians within the women's movement went along with the idea of special interest groups and bedroom issues and didn't talk about their "sexual preference," much less make a political analysis. The Lavender Menace action in the spring of 1970 opened up this oppressive and alienating situation but the feminist movement has been very slow to integrate the lesbian's vision with their ideology and (inter)personal practice.[40]

The paper ends with little hope of working alongside activists in the women's movement.

Both issues, lesbian feminist separatism from straight women and from gay men, received considerable attention in the media and within the women's movement.[41] Lesbian feminist separatism has as much to do with the competing ideas about coalition politics as a kind of movement-based political constituency. When lesbian sexuality took on more analytic and ideological qualities as a feminist issue, the possibility for coalitions between groups and movements grew. With the greater possibility for cross-movement communication, membership, and solidarity, instability over the boundaries of each movement also grew. Lesbian feminist demands for a noncontradictory movement (in politics, issues, membership, and so on) respond to these new conditions. But the purist solutions more often stymied than solved the difficulty of creating lasting coalitions between movements.[42] As Shane Phelan's study of lesbian feminist separatism suggests, they allowed movements to retreat from their most challenging positions and redraw the boundaries in more conservative ways.[43] They parceled out organizational territory and sapped the energy from cross-movement issues. The very contradictions and imperfections of cross-movement politics, I suggest, produce the most dynamic, if often frighteningly unpredictable, possibilities.

THE "LESBIAN" IN "FEMINISM"

The legacy of early articulations of lesbian sexuality as a feminist issue has only begun to be explored by historians and sociologists. Even in the two groups I discuss, Seattle Radical Women and Bread and Roses, the impact is not easy to trace.[44] For while collective documents show what groups wanted to project, they do not uncover fully either how an issue functioned in a group or group dynamics around that issue. However, these interventions paved the way for changes in the women's movement, though all groups did not respond with the same immediacy.

Early on, the left-wing Seattle Radical Women articulates a flamboyant expression of sexuality as a feminist issue:

> End the double standard of sexual morality in all facets of life. Our sexuality and our nature is for us to determine; we define ourselves. Fundamental to the liberation of women is our right as free individuals to exercise control over our own bodies on the basis of our own judgment.[45]

Even before Radicalesbians' high profile action in 1970, Seattle Radical Women upheld women's freedom to define their sexuality. However, paired with the criticism of repressive standards of women's sexual morality, *sexuality* could refer to lesbian sexuality, bisexuality, or just wider definitions of acceptable heterosexual sex. Yet even this ambiguity does not negate the importance of Seattle Radical Women's stand. Seattle Radical Women's position paper announces sweeping demands for women's self-determination in sex, nature, and morality. As issues, these demands could include women's decisions about abortion, procreation, sexual practices, and desire.

However, Seattle Radical Women's position paper of 1972 makes no mention of lesbians or lesbian sexuality.[46] Their earlier ambiguous discussion of sexual freedom for women is not repeated. But in no uncertain terms, the paper advocates "the abolition of the monogamous family as the economic unit of society" in words that mirror Comedy's speech, though *nuclear* and *monogamous* have different inflections.[47] Nuclear describes heterosexual and/or two-parent families, whereas monogamy refers to the sexual relationship within the family, and equates marital sex acts with property relations. None of their position papers from the conference mentions sexuality in general or lesbian sexuality in particular. *Sex* in the title of Dorothy Chambless's paper, "Race and Sex, 1972: Collision or Comradeship?" refers to biological difference only, not sexuality or sex acts.[48] While in their position papers Seattle Radical Women rally against sexist familial structures, they do not assimilate conceptual categories developed by lesbian feminist groups into their analysis or include lesbian sexuality as a feminist issue. In fact, women's sexuality and erotic liberation drop out of their program all together. Only in 1974 does Seattle Radical Women advocate the end of "[p]ersecution of lesbians and homosexuals, based on the threat they pose to the conventional family."[49] The demand solidifies as a discrete issue of civil rights rather than a critique of heteronormativity.

One Boston group within the women's liberation movement, Bread and Roses, develops a feminist critique of sexuality in their early manifesto, one which also does not mention lesbian sexuality or erotic liberation as visualized by Radicalesbians. They state several goals for women's liberation from familial oppression—goals that presume a heterosexual, nuclear family structure:

> A militant women's liberation movement must go on from this point to demand (1) that mothers must also be free in the home, (2) that management must pay for child care facilities so that women can do equal work with men, and that (3) equal work *with* men must mean equal work *by* men (their emphasis).[50]

Even their goals for sexual emancipation involve knowledge about birth control, assuming the erotic liberation of women leads to pregnancy.

Bread and Roses propose a radical feminist agenda, one that treats no issue as a single goal. They attempt to propose reforms that, if won, would build women's participation in revolutionary politics. Their audience would widen with the addition of Radicalesbians' category, sex, and Comedy's analysis of the family. At this point, Bread and Roses' manifesto does not include lesbians or lesbian-feminist critiques of heterosexism and homophobia. This omission in 1969, when their manifesto was published, may not signify a conscious political decision to exclude lesbian sexuality as an issue. Even in a very active city for lesbian feminists, Washington, D.C., just a few months before Joan Comedy spoke to the women's rally, the Forum series for the Women's Liberation Movement course at the Washington Area Free University had no session (out of eleven) on lesbians or lesbian sexuality.[51]

After 1970, however, Bread and Roses recognized the importance of lesbian sexuality as an issue and lesbians as a feminist constituency. The agenda for their conference lists "gay liberation" as a workshop topic for the second day.[52] The opening suggested discussion question raises feminist definitions of *gay* as more than acts or relationships. "What does it mean to identify oneself as gay (particularly as gay women) 1) sexually, 2) in relationship to other women, to men, to 'straight' homosexuality, 3) in relationship to institutions in the U.S."[53] And its last and perhaps most revealing question about the anxiety lesbian sexuality produced as a feminist issue, "Who cares anyway?" The following questions suggest that the definition of gay is something the women's movement must care about. If gay refers to sexual, interpersonal and institutional relations, then the women's movement must rethink its ideological boundaries. Topic number seven points towards this reconceptualization: "How does our women's liberation analysis view the relationship between sexism, male and female roles, and heterosexuality in our society? Are there revolutionary implications of homosexuality? What is the relationship between traditional homosexuality and gay liberation?[54] While the organizers do not state it directly, the order of these questions suggests that men in the gay liberation movement may be very close allies to a nonheterosexist women's movement. Additionally, the second to last question asks about the relationship of an activist's sexuality to their politics, and of sexuality to politics more generally. Homosexuality potentially implicates feminism not just as a movement, but as a theory.

The presence of the gay liberation movement and its relationship to women's liberation permeates many of the discussion questions. Bread and Roses asks participants to think about whether "a particular and/or new politics . . . comes out of the gay movement—different from the women's movement." Another set of questions raises the specter of separatism, "Are there parts of gay consciousness and struggle to be worked out with gay men, or is gay liberation inherently two movements—male and female?"[55] The question of new politics creates the basis for two separate movements, not because men are active in the gay liberation movement, but because they have "particular" politics. Through an ideological difference, the women's movement and the gay liberation movement operate autonomously. Yet the potential for similar goals and a common movement also marks this question. Depending on the emphasis, their question could mean: "*Is* there a difference between the two movements?" Yet when the panel asks about separatism directly, it is about lesbian separatism from a gay men's liberation movement, not from a straight women's movement.

While Bread and Roses frames the questions to challenge stable movement boundaries, they simultaneously minimize their implications for the women's liberation movement. Radical Women, like Bread and Roses, cannot wholly ignore how lesbian sexuality reformulates feminist politics. Nor can they fully contain the rippling implications of the issue. Sex configures feminist politics in ways Koedt could not guess in her early article about orgasms. Likewise, an issue becomes political, and significantly makes politics, in ways no movement can predict or control.

As a site of external, organized struggles, lesbian sexuality could not be contained as a discrete issue within feminism or even within lesbian feminism. As a constitutive part of an active gay liberation movement and as a site of social critique, the issue demanded a more flexible understanding of both gay and women's liberation movements. Struggles around lesbian sexuality, given these conditions, prefigured a coalition between movements and activists. Bernice Reagon Johnson points out in her influential essay "Coalitional Politics: Turning the Century" that coalitions are by definition dangerous. She writes:

> I feel as if I'm gonna keel over any minute and die. That is often what it feels like if you're *really* doing coalition work. Most of the time you feel threatened to the core and if you don't, you're not really doing no coalescing . . . . You don't go into coalition because you just *like* it. The only reason you would consider trying to team up with somebody who could possibly kill you, is because that's the only way you can figure you can stay alive.[56]

Reagon structures coalitional work through struggle and for survival. Yet that survival is not just individual or community-based, but also organizational. Pioneering work by Urvashi Vaid, Biddy Martin and Chandra Mohanty and more recent articles about poststructuralism, feminism, and queer politics stress the centrality of struggle to the regeneration of radical and progressive movements for social change.[57] Strict boundaries, set goals, and definitive answers will stifle creative solutions that inhere even in organized, campaign-based struggles. As Rosa Luxemburg suggests, to envision struggle solely through organizational goals and demands is to see only one side of organizations' politics. Political organization must transform itself through dangerous chances, such as those precarious coalitions that threaten existing formations.

FIVE

STRUGGLE AND THE FEMINIST INTELLECTUAL

The heyday of feminist activism, says common knowledge, is over. Recent feminist theories, in this narrative, mirror an apolitical tendency at large—they are theories of feminism as a set of ideals and critiques, not of the women's movement as a dynamic political force. As Seyla Benhabib asks skeptically, "Can feminist theory be postmodernist and still retain an interest in emancipation?"[1] Feminist theories are apolitical, we are told, because the women's movement has lost its momentum and, as a result, its mandate for feminist thinkers.[2] But present theories of feminism, from conservative to postfoundationalist to materialist, remain deeply political. All of these strands maintain an unwavering commitment to struggle.[3] These contemporary theories of feminism do address issues of struggle in relation to organization, and in this regard they are examples of feminist theories of organizing. None of these positions, however, draws out their organizational assumptions explicitly. In fact, few state their views about feminism as a process of struggle or as an organizational entity.

In his 1956 essay, "Our Struggle," Dr. Martin Luther King illustrates a colloquial, but more complicated, usage of the term struggle.[4] His title, in part, refers to the activism of the civil rights organizers and participants. But his essay also mobilizes a new meaning for the term: the movement for civil rights itself. He writes, "Montgomery has demonstrated that we will not run from the struggle."[5] Using the definite article in "*the* struggle," he refers to the civil rights movement in its complex entirety; as a result, struggle takes on an added significance in the essay's title. "Our struggle" invokes both the battles against racial exploitation and oppression that African Americans, people of color, and all residents of the U.S. must fight, and the movement formed to sustain those battles. *Struggle,* in this heightened sense, alludes to a relationship between the consensus-building and instrumental activity of struggle and political organization. Struggle includes the process of how those minute and daily efforts inform the civil rights movement as a larger entity. Importantly, the term includes *how* that movement can then transform those disparate actions into substantive racial justice. Struggle, in this latter aspect, raises the question that wracked the later civil rights movement: What, organizationally, constitutes an expansive vision of racial justice? Dr. King's insight structures the inquiry of this chapter: How does the incremental activity of struggle, both organized and unorganized, integrate an expansive political vision into the larger entity of political organization? In other words, What are the values of organization we must debate in order to substantiate feminist projections for social transformation? Recent feminist theories usually accord struggle an honorable mention. However, their primary focus on the subject and subjectivity ignores the integral relationship between organization and struggle; what works in feminism, how it works, and what feminism supports. Debates from the mid-sixties to the early seventies illustrate what we have lost when we only discuss the feminist subject and feminist subjectivity. We have lost explicit articulations about vital questions of representation in organization, but also of leadership and interconnection with other political movements (and distinctions from other movements). We have lost the opportunity to debate of feminism even as an ongoing process of resistance and assertion.

Feminist theory from the mid-sixties and early seventies draws a much more visible connection between political programs and strategies. Often, the strategic elements overshadow any definitions of theoretical terms and presuppositions these theories detail. For this reason, political ephemera from this period are usually read as historical documentation of what happened, rather than as information on how these feminists envisioned social, political, and economic change. These documents, I argue, clarify what theoretical assumptions and definitions enabled the emergent movement to relate to the strategies and tactics they employed. Current feminist theories do not typically advertise their political intentions as clearly as Margaret Benston's "The Political Economy of Women's Liberation."[6] Benston wrote her essay in 1969 to chart the terrain for a new movement and to provide an understanding of what already existed in the efforts to organize women. As I argue in chapter 1, in order to analyze the political economy of the women's liberation movement she depends upon a tacit recognition of organization as it mediates theory and practice. Benston, like many of her generation of writers, does not separate her theoretical definition of feminism from strategic and tactical questions of leadership, representation, and the movement's interconnections and separations. Unlike many feminist scholars today, she explicitly addresses those questions of organization. This chapter shifts from her article's content to its production. Women in Action, a small, revolutionary women's group in New York with a primarily black, working-class membership, sharply question Benston's methods, rather than her article's content, as a reflection of what is disturbing in feminist activism. They judge her scholarship, in its production and analysis, as flawed praxis. Their critique never raises any dichotomy between the activist and the scholar, between activism and scholarship. The ethical lucidity of Women in Action's position clarifies how struggle meets organization for the feminist intellectual.

Among contemporary theories of feminism, individualist or liberal theories valorize unorganized aspects of the subject's fight to gain wealth or power, but with an eye toward the institutionalization of individual striving in a collective and unidimensional force.[7] They strongly overemphasize organization to the detriment of struggle. While many liberal feminist theorists are not backed by right-wing foundations, as are many conservative writers about feminism, such as Christine Hoff Sommers, their common focus on the individual in relation to society creates important commonalities in their conclusions and methodologies. One example of their common organizational assumptions is Naomi Wolf's concept of 'power feminism', which celebrates individual feminists who work within the status quo to gain its rewards.[8] Perhaps paradoxically, given their strong individualism, this trend in feminist theory struggles for hegemony among top-down concepts of feminist leadership—one that directs feminism. Postfoundationalist feminist theories display a different imbalance. As I argue in chapter 3, their laudable fight against exclusion, hierarchy, and coercion results in the rejection of organization entirely. Struggle, in postfoundationalist feminism, is not only a means to build a healthy feminism, but an end for it as well.[9] Materialist feminists, in the tradition of Rosa Luxemburg perhaps, propose a more dialectical vision of struggle and organization in feminism.[10] They draw careful ties between theory and practice in feminism, giving primacy neither to political action, as some unadulterated enactment of beliefs, nor to those articulations of what feminism is, can be, or should become. None of these writers, perhaps not surprisingly, discounts the role of the feminist scholar in her proposal(s) for a better feminist movement. Each accords feminist scholars very different positions in that struggle for regeneration (or hegemony).

What interests me in reading disparate feminist theorists' ongoing commitment to struggle is how they negotiate the term's central concerns of process, flux, and interconnection in feminism. As such theorists as Patricia Huntington and Kathi Weeks astutely observe, these dynamic aspects of intersubjectivity and the contextual specificities of social change raise neglected questions of value in politics that critiques (and countercritiques) of foundationalism so often ignore.[11] Theories that address how we assign value in politics simultaneously question those feminist politics that are based on the slippage of meaning and discursive resignification. Huntington argues against this aspect of unspecified value in Judith Butler's theory of discursive agency that I discuss in detail in chapter 3. She writes, "[T]he nature of the deliberate, self-regulating moment in this positive and productive activity, whereby we critically differentiate between nondominating and repressive, feminist and masculinist forms of adopting an alternative script among those in competition for our identities, is left unspecified."[12] As reactive practices, many postfoundationalist feminists refuse to ask what specific resignifications may produce or how these slippages may change existing relations. Both Weeks and Huntington show how discussions about value in politics emphasize the positive aspects of political transformation and building something new rather than the reactive capacity of political values. The concept of struggle does not necessarily admit questions of value in political resistance. But in relation to the concerns of organization, of how theory meets practice, any discussion about struggle must wrestle with value in relation to tactical, strategic, and what Huntington calls "utopic," or long-term goals.

THEORETICAL POLITICS

Current writings about feminism that touch on issues of organization and struggle are couched in the language of theory and practice. The terms, stakes, and contexts of these debates have changed dramatically since the early seventies. But theoretical and political commonalities still connect these articulations about feminism. Catalytic questions remain about who leads the movement for progressive/Leftist change, which movements enervate or support other struggles, and where distinctions between movements lie. *Practice* and *theory* are not parallel terms to *struggle* and *organization*. *Practice* does, however, encompass many of the instrumental aspects of struggle, while *theory* can include issues of organization in its purview. In a marked departure from earlier writings, the concerns of the subject and subjectivity now dictate the course of debates about leadership, representation, and interconnection in feminism. To paraphrase Linda Alcoff's assumption, for the last twenty years the subject has been considered the starting point for any politics.[13] This is true even of postfoundationalist theories that dismantle a humanist subject in politics. As the dominant concern of debates about feminism, the subject has replaced early second wave attention to institutionalized organization.

In recent discussions about feminism, even this subject-centered negotiation of theory and practice has been pronounced irrelevant (or long rent asunder) by critics of feminism. They stress the shortcomings of theory or practice in the abstract, or in feminisms' particulars. Feminist analyses exacerbate the hostile misreadings and appropriation of feminism by ignoring the connections between theory and practice. Aging New Leftists have attacked the U.S. women's movement as a pesky identity-based diversion to the unifying stimuli of a purely class-based politics.[14] Right-wing and liberal critics have characterized feminist theory as loaded with jargon and fatally out of touch with politics on the ground.[15] In this vein, Christina Hoff Sommers answers the by-now familiar question of why young women do not call themselves feminists. In an article for the libertarian-capitalist *American Enterprise,* she writes, "Most girls now reject the feminist label because today's feminism is proving so irrelevant and useless to average women."[16] But this analysis of feminism and (potential) feminists ignores many examples of feminist theory that are guided by political concerns.

None of the critics of identity politics, from Todd Gitlin to Sommers, points to another field of analysis other than a politics of identity—though they prefer to keep their identity politics unnamed. Gitlin's argument rests upon recentering a truncated working-class agenda, one that supercedes identities based on race or gender.[17] He proposes a new subject of labor politics, one unmarked, or at least prior to other identities. For Sommers, the identity politics of the individual (a category without further definition) is implicitly a category of privilege, or at the very least of the status quo. Sommer's individual, produced within a capitalist democracy, has preconditions of privilege and resources that her argument ignores. Both Sommers's and Gitlin's alternatives to identity politics stay within the logic of identity politics. Gitlin makes a claim for solidarity and progressive change, while

Sommers emphatically does not, but both merely assert an alternative subject for politics. Both critiques rest upon identity as the starting point for politics. But both positions quite baldly demand that we ask who leads, on whose terms, to what ends. Just as bluntly, both New Leftists and liberal-individualist feminists provide their own answers to these questions.

Neither materialist nor postfoundationalist feminists abdicate responsibility either for questions of theory and practice in feminism, or for definitions of organization and strategy for feminism. While their responses are often phrased in terms antagonistic to each other, or only partially allied, both directly confront organizational demands of feminism. Postfoundationalist critiques, such as Butler's, tear down any foundationalist basis for the subject in politics. They suggest alternate models for autonomy, separatism, and interconnections in feminism. They criticize the sexism, homophobia, and racism of the New Leftists' charges against identity politics and individualist feminists' abject surrender to the status quo. But postfoundationalist theories of organizing through politicized, shifting identities are still mired in the precepts and the limitations of an antisubject/subject dichotomy. Materialist feminists, such as Weeks, Huntington, and Teresa Ebert, begin to supercede the focus on the subject through long-term and systemic analyses of feminism. They propose more complex and thorough understandings of how feminism can operate as a movement in relation to other movements. They suggest how political formations substantiate feminist theories. Ebert most clearly fleshes out how self-critique in feminism can guide the movement. She argues that no limited conception of unity, or sisterhood, can bind feminist politics or feminist theory together. Instead, Ebert argues, feminism can proceed only through a dialectical relationship between theory and practice which formalizes struggle in organization and respects the logic of disparate struggles. However, despite these significant differences, both materialist and postfoundationalist arguments about feminism undermine liberal and conservative visions of feminism. To understand these antagonists also helps to elaborate the range of alternatives that theorists such as Ebert and Butler propose. Likewise, right-wing critics position an individualist feminism against postfoundationalism and materialism. This debate over feminism structures my argument for a dialectical conception of the relationship of struggle to organization.

Sommers's limited assessment of what constitutes feminism overestimates the importance of organization vis-à-vis struggle. In her assessment of feminism as irrelevant to women, Sommers assumes that the "feminist label" rejected by girls reflects the state of feminism as a whole: for Sommers, there is no political economy of women's liberation *because* young women do not call themselves feminist. Political organization, or the women's movement, dictates struggle, or the self-identification (or lack thereof) of people to that movement. If young women don't identify with feminism, she argues, the fault lies with political organization alone. In her book *Who Stole Feminism?* Sommers cites statistics which reveal most young women's support for a strong women's movement to fight for women's equal rights and equal pay. Even in the face of this evidence, she draws the assumption

that feminism is a movement dying a natural death, though she simultaneously credits its demise to the favorable conditions faced by women in the United States.[18]
She blames the current intellectual leadership, feminist academics:

> In effect, the gender feminists lack a grass roots constituency. They blame a
> media "backlash" for the defection of the majority of women. But what happened
> is clear enough: the gender feminists have stolen "feminism" from a mainstream
> that had never acknowledged their leadership.[19]

Women who identify as feminists are identical to feminism. In Sommers's logic,
when they fail to identify themselves as feminists, the movement has lost its membership. And further, leaders define feminism, so this failure of identification is due
to their poor leadership. Struggle, or what people do, is immaterial to her definition of feminism. Instead, objective oppression and exploitation based on gender
and the leader-centered character of political organization determine the fate of
struggle.

Sommers's top-down conception of feminism is little concerned with the in-
tersectionality of movements and struggles, and primarily concerned with leadership. As her bibliography starkly illustrates, Sommers reads little feminist scholarship about race, sexuality, or class. Her term for that derelict feminism rejected by
young women is *gender feminism*. In her definition, gender feminism attempts to
be only about gender, or to use Joan Scott's definition of gender, only about sexual difference. This strict segmentation is equally true for Sommers's definition of
a more palatable feminism, one she connects to the first wave of feminism: equity
feminism. She defines equity feminism as a movement for "fair treatment, without
discrimination."[20] As, in her view, equity feminism remains strictly distinct
(through ideology and chronology) from gender feminism, Sommers breaks any potential continuity or connection between the two.

Sommers portrays gender feminism as made up of leaders who lack a grassroots
constituency. Though decrying a movement purportedly without adherents, she defines leader vaguely at best. Even if a leader merely mobilizes people, rather than
organizing them (say, to identify as feminists)—a definition of top-down leadership—someone must be mobilized. Sommers is disingenuous in her critique of gender feminism since her real concern does not lie with the grass roots, but with feminism's leaders and a feminism that leads. Primarily on the basis of its leadership,
Sommers argues, gender feminism is a wrong-headed and formidable (if often fool-
ish) enemy. She is most alarmed by the heavy-handed and, in her view, fatally misguided changes won by gender feminists in public policy and education. Particularly telling in this regard is her statement about women's studies: "[E]quipping
students to 'transform the world' is not quite the same as equipping them with the
knowledge they need for getting on in the world."[21] Young women in college, she
infers through sarcasm, should learn how to work the system, not challenge it. Any
feminist would agree these are different goals. But since Sommers conceives political organization without any consideration of struggle, feminism is primarily

a question of leadership by the movement. She does not give any serious consideration to the demands of a diverse and multidirectional constituency in shaping the demands of that movement. Instead, she hopes to redefine the purpose of feminism so that, from the top down, feminism can direct the goals and aspirations of young women to be more reformist, less combative. A feminism that organizes rather than leads or advocates for women is much too threatening. Leadership (and control of that leadership) of feminism is Sommers's aim in retheorizing feminism as a political formation.

Judith Butler's response to Nancy Fraser's book *Justice Interruptus,* entitled "Merely Cultural," proposes a very different feminism from that of Sommers. Butler's argument, for instance, lacks any consideration of leadership. Instead, semi-autonomy and self-differentiation explode strictly delimited definitions of feminism as an organizational entity. The proliferation of struggles overrides any concern with their formalization or institutionalization. Butler's ethical concern in this argument is exclusion—any exclusion of struggle from feminism. She frames her argument as one against the limiting confines of what constitutes radical politics for New Leftists and, to some degree, for Nancy Fraser. Butler attacks the subtle chipping away of New Leftist politics cognizant of gender, race, and sexuality, rather than Fraser's argument specifically. Butler faults the zero-sum exclusion which sustains the arguments by Todd Gitlin and Richard Rorty, among others, in her scathing rebuttal to New Leftists (and, almost tangentially, Fraser). When Gitlin and others argue that sexuality, race, or gender are purely (and merely) an identity, unconnected to reformist class issues, they exclude recognition of anything but their own truncated conception of class. While Butler highlights the exclusion of queer studies, relegated to the secondary realm of the merely cultural, gender and race are also considered largely matters of identity particularism by these New Leftists' class critique. Separatism, to Gitlin et al., is a threat, as are all permutations of struggles not overtly marked by class.

In a recent article, Gitlin characterized the problem facing the Left as one of "how to transcend the divisiveness of identity politics."[22] He argues in favor of the transcendence of division within Left politics without ever examining the New Left's well-documented history of homophobia, sexism, and racism.[23] The problem, in the view of Gitlin, Eric Alterman, and Rorty, lies in how gender, race, or sexuality frame movements, not in the specific context of their political organization or current social conditions. In this sense, the fault for division lies solely with deluded social actors who misunderstand their own interests and the interests of progressive struggle.

In her response, Butler describes "the tendency to relegate new social movements to the sphere of the cultural, indeed, to dismiss them as being preoccupied with what is called the 'merely' cultural, and then to construe this cultural politics as factionalizing, identitarian, and particularistic."[24] She describes a logic, one she calls exclusionary and violent, wherein the cultural has less value as it translates into politics. Butler's disagreement does not stem from the depreciation of new social movements alone, but also from the demotion of these politics' value through their description as "cultural." Because Butler refuses to name the culprits, her characterization encompasses the Left much more generally, and by default includes Fraser and, indeed, almost anyone who has criticized identity politics.[25]

Butler's position has an additional aspect, one that speaks more directly to Fraser's carefully wrought argument. The cultural is also a kind of politics, one more diffuse, less movement-directed than either the politics of recognition or redistribution as described by Fraser. Butler describes new social movements, or, more specific to her argument, queer studies, as "semi-autonomous." In keeping with her test case of queer studies, she likens this semi-autonomy to new disciplines on race, religion, gender, and sexuality. Butler writes:

> Within the academy, the effort to separate race studies from sexuality studies from gender studies marks various needs for autonomous articulation, but it also invariably produces a set of important, painful, and promising confrontations that expose the ultimate limits to any such autonomy: the politics of sexuality within African-American studies, the politics of race within queer studies, within the study of class, within feminism, the question of misogyny within any of the above, the question of homophobia within feminism, to name a few.[26]

The semi-autonomy that Butler describes is one of "needs," though her definition of needs is not clear. She could refer to needs inherent in the struggle of queer studies and sexuality more generally, a reading at odds with her militant antiessentialism. More likely, Butler refers to an institutional limit which demands a separatist articulation of gender and race in order to form a seemingly cohesive field of study.[27] Although modeled in form on area studies, these programs, which grew out of youth activism of the sixties and seventies, have a very different internal logic. The reformist limits of the academy are overdetermined by the character of this kind of (inter)disciplinary intervention into college curricula. To intervene through a particular socioeconomic category, like gender or sexuality, will also raise questions of race and religion, among others. Another possibility, raised by Butler's use of the plural "various needs," is a reference to the awkward combination of the inherent demands of a movement (represented in this passage by queer, African-American, and women's studies) and the reformist translation of a revolutionary movement into the academy.

This semi-autonomy of new social movements is not specific to the academy, for Butler, but describes new social movements' more general character. As such, semi-autonomy also marks the interconnectedness between particularist struggles, presumably including class-based struggles. Semi-autonomy proffers the likelihood of each movement's own transformation, whether through diffusion with other struggles, or in response to changes in the political landscape. The unstable character of a new social movement, in particular, allows Butler to conceive of a movement defined by "*the self-difference of movement itself,*" a constitutive rupture that makes movements possible on non-identitarian grounds, that installs a certain mobilizing conflict as the basis of politicization"(emphasis in original).[28]

Semi-autonomy in this sense is set in opposition to the New Leftist unity which rigidifies struggles through boundaries and a homogeneity established from above.

Also part of self-difference is the process of leadership, deciding what should remain part of a movement or group, and what must change. As a critical process, self-difference in Butler's model is a method for making these difficult decisions in a movement. She assumes that productive dissent will self-correct problems in movements or disciplines, but does not give any indication of how this will happen, or how it will happen without some conscious exclusion of one trend, faction, formation, ideology, or another. Dissent, even self-differentiating dissent, has exclusionary consequences. And, whether decided upon by a collective or through a de facto or a representative leadership, the outcomes of self-difference cannot remain wholly unconscious or natural to politics.

Butler's distaste for political organization, represented in a crude way by her description of unity, has an urgent tone in this article:

> The problem of unity, or more modestly of solidarity, cannot be resolved through the transcendence or obliteration of this field (identity-based political formations), and certainly not through the vain promise of retrieving a unity wrought through exclusions, one that reinstitutes subordination as the condition of its own possibility. The only possible unity will not be the synthesis of a set of conflicts, but will be *a mode of sustaining conflict in politically productive ways.*[29] (emphasis in original)

In this passage, Butler does not fully renounce unity but connects the arguments of Gitlin et al. to all stable unities, a quality of unity she equates with exclusion and subordination. Butler attempts to resolve her own antiorganizational position through the contingency of struggle. The unity of a semi-autonomous movement must forever succumb to the shifting relationships between movements and struggles, never asserting its politics except as relational positions to struggle with each other. But unity and organization, as problems of politics, cannot simply be transmuted into struggle. The question remains of how particular sites of struggle, such as the fight over academic disciplines, relate to a larger political formation, whether queer politics or progressive politics. Butler avoids any question of leadership as such in new social movements: this is an issue, I argue, suppressed in antiorganizational positions more generally.

In contrast to Butler, who questions feminist categories of analysis, and New Leftists' limited definitions of feminism, Teresa Ebert changes the purview and scope of debates about feminism. Ebert frames her discussion of feminism with wider questions of political organization. She states, "I am writing to reclaim historical materialism for feminism in post-modernity and to contribute to the construction of a revolutionary theory and praxis for third-wave feminism—new red feminism."[30] Often through language and concepts difficult to access, she attempts to link "high theory" abstractions to larger political visions and consequences. Ebert provides a political economy of the third wave, and launches her trenchant critique of conservative tendencies in feminist theory in order to build toward a revolutionary movement, one she calls "red feminism."

Ebert repeats two themes throughout the first chapter. First, she seeks to clarify the importance of historical materialism for emerging feminists and a revitalized women's movement. Second, she situates her theory as a productive critique of trends in feminist analyses, a critique enabling political transformation, not resignification. Both of these themes have organizational repercussions. Her methodological commitment to historical materialism leads her to a very different conception of the relationship of feminism to other movements for social change. Her focus on particular kinds of transformation as feminist reframes debates about leadership in feminism as a movement and an ethical commitment. In both of her main themes Ebert resuscitates the early second wave question of how to build a revolutionary, rather than a reformist, movement. For Ebert, "the revolutionary socialist feminist . . . always insists that the material is fundamentally tied to the economic sphere and to the relations of production, which have a historically necessary connection to all other social-cultural relations."[31] When Ebert advocates feminist transformation, she simultaneously militates for the eradication of exploitation in the social totality.

Ebert's definition of historical materialism, in contrast to what she calls the "matterism" of present definitions of materialist feminism, is a marxist mode of critique. The scope of historical materialism and the realm of critique in theory are strikingly similar to organization as a methdological category in Lukács and Luxemburg.[32] According to Ebert:

> Historical materialist critique is that knowledge practice that historically situates the possibility of what exists under patriarchal capitalist relations of difference— particularly the division of labor—and points to what is suppressed by the empirically existing: not just what *is*, but what could be. . . . The role of critique. . . . is exactly this: the production of historical knowledges that marks the transformability of existing social arrangements and the possibility of a different social organization—an organization free from exploitation.[33](emphasis in original)

In Ebert's definition of critique, theory is never divorced from practice; it is intimately connected to the possibilities of political intervention and struggle. An historically materialist critique must not only make the connections between phenomenon and experiences, to flesh out those unseen interrelationships, but also must produce theoretico-practical possibilities for change. This insistence on building an analysis of the social totality, as a means of strengthening politics, exemplifies Ebert's commitment to the process of making our knowledge/experience conscious. That is, critique functions here much like organization in Lukács's and Luxemburg's writings. Organization is always implicated in the conditions of its possibility and the vision it seeks to embody. In this sense, Ebert proposes a conception of the women's movement, or a political movement in general, radically different from that posed by either Sommers or Butler. Unlike in Butler's view, the political movement is not a collection of self-differentiating struggles; unlike in Sommers's view, even this more formal notion of movement does not, in itself, lead struggles.

The process of making struggle conscious through critique is exactly that— an ongoing process, defined not so much by what the movement is at any given moment, but by what Ebert calls a "movement engaged in self-critique." This process of self-critique demands constant renegotiation of the political struggles at hand, of the analyses of the social totality, and of the projections for what can be and how to effect those changes. Through her concept of self-critique, Ebert is able to define feminism not as a movement guided by the demands of unity, figured as the unadulterated politics of class by Gitlin et al., but as a movement which includes the formalization both of struggle through theory, and of struggle as disparate battles. Ebert asserts, "If feminism, as an ensemble of contesting ways of knowing and political practices, is to continue to develop, it must be self-critical. It needs to understand that a materialist critique of its own historical situation and limits is vital to its ongoing struggle against patriarchy."[34] In superficial ways, this self-critical aspect, resembles Butler's argument for a productively self-differentiating feminist movement. But Ebert, unlike Butler, never skirts the issue of this self-critical component to a movement-based struggle against capitalism and patriarchy. The demands of these collectivized struggles inform the self-critical feminist movement, not the self-differentiating one. Organization, even in this aspect, is ever present.

Ebert's reliance on the demands of organization in relation to struggle may seem synonymous with Sommers's determinist overemphasis on the movement's leadership of women. But unlike Ebert, who projects organization as a limit of struggle, for Sommers political organization (its character, membership, etc.) *is* struggle. In Sommers's view, organization does not make struggle conscious through the formalization of its insights and tools, but produces struggle through correct theory (in Sommers's argument, equity feminism). Through Ebert's concept of a self-critical movement as a movement of process and regeneration through dissent, she avoids Sommers's static conception of the movement as a political practice and as a movement with discrete boundaries.

Both of the issues highlighted by Sommers and Butler, leadership and interconnection of movement/struggle respectively, are implicit in Ebert's argument as well. However, for Ebert, neither leadership nor interconnection resolves the contradictions between struggle and organization. Instead, Ebert links these issues dialectically, since leadership and movements' interconnection contain limits of both organization and struggle. Ebert argues that it is precisely the interconnections between struggles that must inform feminism's embrace of class politics. "Feminism," she observes, "needs to go beyond its own contemporary limits and include class in its struggle."[35] Feminism, through a more complicated inclusion of related struggles, also produces an exclusion of struggles. That is, in order to fight exploitative relations of production, feminism must reject elitist and racist battles for women through a renewed commitment to class politics. This interconnection, between the politics of gender and the politics of class, does not answer Butler's concern about a violently exclusionary unity, though it does address her concern with breaking down rigid and separatist definitions of feminism.

Interconnection, in Ebert's thesis, is simultaneously an argument for political leadership by the women's movement. The feminist movement, by building class alliances between struggles, takes the initiative to reject particular strategies employed under the guise of feminism, such as an undifferentiated goal of adding to the number of women in managerial positions. Interconnection, in this sense, means building a political leadership to exclude particular struggles from the rubric of feminism. With certain distinctions, Ebert builds more on theories of the revolutionary women's movement from the late sixties and early seventies than on present theories of the political economy of the women's movement.

AUTONOMY, SEMI-AUTONOMY, AND INTERCONNECTION OF MOVEMENTS

To understand the historical and theoretical weight of interconnection and separatism in the formation of feminism, we must look back a little farther than debates from the nineties. Feminist theories about organizing give much more weight to questions about interconnection than to questions about feminism's distinctiveness. But questions regarding interconnection and coalition rest upon assumptions about differentiation between struggles and movements. Autonomy and separatism lie at the heart of calls for linking politics together. Even Sommers, whose argument in favor of equity feminism depends upon hermetically sealed movements for equity and gender feminism, only infers an implicit, methodological break between the two. Autonomy, as Alice Echols confirms in her history of radical feminism, once conjured up images of self-determination and of a means to build leadership and power among historically disenfranchised people.[36] The idea of autonomy was intended to produce a more focused movement, unified by struggles both more narrowly defined and pursuing more coherent goals. The slogan of the Black Power movement, exhorting activists to fight their own battles, forged a close alliance between personal experience and social oppression in the form of the autonomy of political struggles.[37] The success of decolonization movements in Asia and Africa strengthened the link between the organizational form of autonomy and the political goal of a quasi-nationalist self-determination.[38] Within the emerging women's liberation movement, many feminists argued that to support a separate movement was to be fully loyal to women.[39] Historians such as Alice Echols have convincingly illustrated how the sexism rampant in the student and antiwar movements led to the formation of a separate movement for women's liberation.[40] But the push for an autonomous and semi-autonomous women's movement was not a purely reactive demand. Sara Evans documents the importance of the Vietnamese Communist Party, and the National Liberation Front (NLF), which gave a revolutionary edge to the semi-autonomous and autonomous organization of women.[41] Even while Vietnamese women fought in combat, they organized through a semi-autonomous women's group to combat sexism and to push for women's demands within the NLF.

Breakaway groups from the youth and student movements also hoped to develop a more responsive movement for women and not just to pressure the progressive movement as a whole. In part, though, in a movement for the more open-ended goal of liberation, autonomy signified a means to shore up power against civic institutions and the progressive movements at large.[42] Beverly Jones and Judith Brown articulated one of the earliest arguments for a fully autonomous women's movement, one discontinuous with other movements. Women, they argue, "must resist pressure to enter into movement activities other than their own."[43] Part of the demand for autonomy was the wholesale transformation of practices within progressive organizing, such as Jones and Brown's support for structurelessness, which I discussed in chapter 3. In a related trajectory, autonomy also moved toward a more radical break with Left politics and a sexist mainstream—toward alternative communities rather than combative political change.[44]

The degree to which the women's movement was imagined as a wholly autonomous movement was a highly contentious issue, even within women's liberation groups, in the late sixties and early seventies.[45] For many activists, to imagine a separatist movement around the category woman was highly arrogant. To visualize a movement that organized around the singular social category woman or gender ignored the important lessons learned during the fifties and early sixties about building strong coalitions between groups, constitutive interests, and memberships. Women active in the Black Power movement, the student movement, the civil rights movement, and Left parties initially rejected early attempts to create a wholly separate women's movement.[46]

Autonomy is not merely a question of a pro-women, or an anti-men, breakaway (as it was cast in the sixties), or of group ideology, but of organizational structure in relation to political goals. The alternative to full autonomy was a semi-autonomous relationship to larger movements. Characterized by Echols as politicos, the activists who supported the semi-autonomy of the women's movement explicitly cast their political commitments as "revolutionary." Unlike Jones and Brown, who describe the new techniques of the women's movement as a means to confront leftist men's sexism, such activists as Pat Robinson, Joan Jordan, and Marianne Weathers, among others, took a larger view of the problem. They asked how a group/movement could "open itself up to the bottom" in its very structures and procedures. "The bottom" could mean, more generally, the unorganized; it could also mean the most oppressed and exploited people, who are usually swept aside. Arguments for semi-autonomy, as opposed to intramovement caucuses and even autonomy, spoke to this organizational concern.

One early example of this trend was the women's caucus of the Student Non-Violent Coordinating Committee (SNCC), formed in the early part of 1968, which broke away from SNCC that year to expand its scope for organizing third world women.[47] This group was first called the Black Women's Alliance, then the Third World Women's Alliance (TWWA), which I discuss briefly in chapter 2.

Another example is the work by Socialist Workers Party (SWP) members Joan Jordan and Patricia Robinson, who, on different sides of the country, formed groups autonomous from the SWP and semi-autonomous from the progressive movement as a whole. They shared their ideas through letters, articles, and occasional visits.[48] Their visions for semi-autonomy and autonomy centered on how to build a women's movement which was revolutionary in its organizational form and content.

The drive for a revolutionary movement emphasized the relationship of a women's movement to social totality, but also to other political movements fighting for revolution. One widely circulated leaflet by TWWA describes a popular vision of a revolutionary women's movement in concert with third world, civil rights, and workers' struggles.[49] The framework of revolution confronts the women's movement as one political formation among many, a movement principally held together by the categories women and woman. The goals of the movement, as well as its tactics and analyses of social totality, construct politics through gender, albeit a politics that interacts continually with politics informed by race and by class. As the TWWA paper describes this vision, "We recognize the right of all people to be free. As women, we recognize that our struggle is against an imperialist sexist system that oppresses all minority peoples as well as exploiting the majority."[50] A revolutionary movement, in this conception, is never fully autonomous from other revolutionary movements. The formation of a movement around gender or race is one means to strengthen the larger visions of revolution. Movement, in this theory of organizing women, does not signify rejection of other movements for revolutionary change, but a partial unity in the larger social context of revolution.

The revolutionary women's movement, however, is still a movement with separate strategies, constituencies, and campaigns. The Third World Women's Alliance positioned itself in relation to other revolutionary organizations as a means to affect changes in their functioning. One of their demands is as follows:

> That all organizations and institutions (including all so-called radical, militant and/or so-called revolutionary groups) deal with third world women in their own right as human beings and individuals rather than as property of men and only valued in relationship to their association or connection with some man.[51]

The revolutionary women's movement, as part of the entire revolutionary movement, demands that feminism become the ideological prerogative of the movement as a whole. Antisexism is not the fight of women against men, but is integral to the fight for revolutionary changes.

A separate women's movement for revolutionary change also transformed the valence of women in the wider revolutionary struggles. As the articles by TWWA attest, a central demand of women's liberation was the full integration of women into all groups, not a taylorization or ghettoization of particular struggles.[52] TWWA sought entrance and full participation in the struggle for national liberation, as well as a shift in focus from the gender only politics of a separatist feminist movement.

Feminist theories of a semi-autonomous women's movement recognized the structural dynamics between categories of race and class as well as gender—privileging the process and determinants of exploitation, rather than one category. For these theories, diversity among women has a structural basis in capitalism. Neither in organizational nor in theoretical terms could gender be conceived as the only or even the primary bond of political unity. As early as 1966, advocates of the organization of women were strictly enjoined to remember its wider scope:

> If the white [women's] groups do not realize that they are in fact fighting capitalism and racism, we do not have common bonds. If they do not realize the reasons for their condition lie in the system and not simply that men get a vicarious pleasure from "consuming their bodies for exploitative reasons," then we cannot unite with them.[53]

In this passage, Francis Beale, a member of SNCC's women's group and later founding member of TWWA, emphasizes that a structural analysis of women's oppression in the United States cannot omit the class dynamics of capitalism nor oppressive relations of racism.

Beale criticizes the voluntarism of many early feminist analyses of sexism, which argue that men either exploit women naturally, because they cannot help themselves, or because oppressing women is inherently fun. In her essay, Beale rejects arguments about genetics and "doing it because they can" as more than just politically naive. These facile explanations obscure the reproduction of sexism in a complex network of relations that also depend on racialized oppression and class exploitation. Moreover, these explanations create specific political responses that ignore and reinforce the American system of racist capitalism, since the organization of women is limited to fighting the production of the sexist subject. When gender takes analytical precedence over categories of class and race, Beale states, even strategic cross-race and cross-class unity is impossible. Sexism, viewed as part of a system, cannot be combated alone or wholly within subject formation.

In addition, Beale's position represents the view that the response to racism and elitism must be part of the organizational fabric mobilizing the political category, woman. To that end, Marianne Weathers, also a member of TWWA, theorized a semi-autonomous organization of women:

> Women's Liberation should be considered as a strategy for an eventual tie-up with the entire revolutionary movement consisting of women, men and children. We are now speaking of a real revolution (armed). . . . Viet Nam is simply a matter of time and geography.[54]

Competing theories for the organization of women define a feminism open to differences between women and sensitive to changing political contingencies. The collective subject of organization cannot be detected in the details of what a woman is in any empirical sense, but in how the movement can substantiate her strength through collective politics. For Weathers, women's liberation is a distinctive call for social change and a separate movement that circulates in ways contingent on its strength within the revolutionary movement and as one part of the larger terrain of political forces. Women's liberation is political in the same way that it is theoretical, as a constantly changing organizational entity.

MARGARET BENSTON AND WOMEN IN ACTION

By 1966 there were several well-established, even hegemonic, theories of women's organization that propose alternative facets to struggle. While these theories differ on questions of the relative autonomy of women's groups around constituencies and issues and their relation to larger progressive movements for social change, among other things, they share several components. They agree that working-class women, particularly women of color, should lead the movement. Also, they argue that issues faced by the more oppressed women should direct the movement's political energy. Leadership and decision-making policies combine in their support for a structural analysis of women's differential oppression within the relations of an imperialist and racist capitalism. The alternative to a static and predetermined sisterhood-as-feminism depends upon creative theories of leadership and decision-making processes that value, rather than efface, dissent within woman and women's movement.

In 1968, the organizer and psychoanalyst Patricia Robinson was a member of Women in Action and of the SWP, and had been involved in Black Women Enraged in the New York City metropolitan area. Robinson, a black woman, wrote a letter to another SWP member, a white woman named Joan Jordan.[55] The letter is a stinging indictment of the women's movement. Robinson describes the escalating elitism in the movement through the treatment of her group, Women in Action, by Margaret Benston, who wrote "The Political Economy of Women's Liberation." According to Robinson, Benston expressed interest in Women in Action's views after reading its article entitled "Poor Black Women."[56] Robinson does not specify where Benston read the article, although by 1970 it was published in most collections on the women's movement. Originally it seems to have been hand copied from a letter (dated September 11, 1968) addressed to the Black Unity Party of Peekskill, New York. Women in Action's piece outlines a now-familiar position about women's reproductive rights as a wider issue of women's control over her reproductive choices and access to a full range of health resources. They articulate a position that responds to weaknesses in the women's movement's focus on abortion rights and to Black Nationalist demands that black women stop using birth control. Members of the group painstakingly responded by letter to Benston's queries about the character of the struggle for women's liberation. In their letter, they stress the importance of a mass movement, one diverse in its membership and methods: "[O]ne does not constrain himself or keep himself to one class, but you learn to be flexible, that is say, [. . . .] the poor may have different ways of doing and teaching, much of which can benefit the middle class. In this way we call all grow together and understand each other more, and together we can do what has to be done."[57] Benston never wrote back, nor did she acknowledge their contributions to her article. Their vision of a movement respectful of diverse kinds of knowledge and expression is not mentioned in Benston's discussion of the women's liberation movement.

Robinson's letter to Jordan discusses a singular occasion of scholarly and political neglect, but Robinson draws larger conclusions from the one-sided relationship. She states:

> [M]y sisters had been rejected and that is far more dangerous to the movement, the chance to form a party, a black women's movement which will eventually ally itself with white women. . . . I see our party coming from practice and made up of those who have been the activists and have become thinkers and carry both abilities. . . . I also know from experience that the women's movement had damn well better open itself up to the bottom.[58]

Using an analysis and vision difficult to understand today, Robinson outlines an organizational failure of the women's movement. Firstly, she argues that most white feminist organizers and theorists, while they support separate organization of women from men, shun the strategy of organizing black women and women of color semi-autonomously from white women. Instead, they favor a universal women's movement. Secondly, these feminists do not give weight to the accrued political knowledge of daily struggle within diverse constituencies who are involved in myriad facets of political organization: groups that may not be called "feminist." The limited conception of universal sisterhood and an autonomous movement failed to build a dynamic category, struggle, in relation to organization. Those practices and those knowledges that did not fit the mold of what was women's liberation, did not cease to exist because they were ignored. Instead, women's liberation as a movement was impoverished.[59]

The political economy of Benston's article on the women's liberation movement showed the limitations of revolutionary intentions without respect for revolutionary practices. In the fabric of this article's production lay the unequal relations between women, relations also part of the women's movement's collective category, woman. Robinson charges Benston not with sloppiness or even overt racism, but with opportunism: "Benston is dedicated to arid research and is in competition for HEAD women in whatever women's movement arises."[60] Benston writes to reach the attention of leaders, often defined by their relationship to cultural and economic capital. This movement, even at the most delicate and hopeful moments of its beginning, had to build the alternate structures of its own possibility.

Refreshingly, Robinson confirms that her anger stems from the content and process of the article, not its difficult language: "[I]n spite of the above I was very glad to see an article on women's lib. in *Monthly Review* and did expect, after all a fairly erudite approach."[61] Benston accepts the given relations of power when she ignores the input of experienced working-class black activists. Benston does not seek to build alternate channels of analysis or communication through her article, but seeks to reach those already positioned to take leadership in the emerging movement. According to Benston, feminism in its majority (and increasingly hegemonic) form does not stifle black women's access to an increasingly white- and middle-class-dominated movement, since black women can join the movement. More importantly, in Robinson's analysis, black and working-class women are denied access to the power to change and direct this movement, due to an elitist and racist definition of struggle.[62] These women can join the movement, but only under the aegis of other leaders. Robinson's assessment refutes most histories of the early second wave feminist movement.[63] Activists who organized women of color around working-class issues did not reject the women's movement; instead, the very structures reproducing the women's movement increasingly rejected them. By 1968, the growing women's movement did not accept the precepts of struggle and commitments to organization necessary for a movement that could, in Robinson's words, "open itself up to the bottom."

Many early Left feminists in the United States, like Robinson and Jordan, supported the theory that a vanguard of working-class women should lead the feminist movement and, in some arguments, the entire range of Leftist movements.[64] Others believed that women should organize black women, white women, working-class black women: that is, organize women's groups semi-autonomously from each other around categories of race and class to build leadership and strength among exploited and oppressed groups. Neither of these positions view cultural, economic, racial, political, or sexual differences as a strategic end in itself. Representative of many Left feminists, Robinson does not naturalize race or gender in her theories of women's political organization.

Joan Jordan theorizes an explicitly antiessentialist method of organizing women. Jordan, who was a member of such groups as Mothers Alone Working (MAW) and Women Inc., a women's caucus in the Western Pulp and Paper Workers Union in Antioch, California, as well as a members of SWP, organized middle- and working-class white women. She also worked actively with women's liberation groups in the Bay Area and tried to develop links between them and members of Women Inc. In early 1967, Jordan wrote to Pat Robinson, critical about the use of gender as the primary or sole unifying source in a revolutionary women's movement. She stresses the limitations of this method when building a broader organization:

> Of course we will try to win over as many [men] as we can. . . . But there will be many who will attack us. The astute Black Nationalist who knows the value of unity based on color or nationalism will also understand its limits and drawbacks. . . . and will be looking at later stages of the struggle when, as it broadens, alliances have been established between other sections of the oppressed. . . . Revolutionary women's organizations that have developed their own *leadership,* authority and program. . . . will have the organized POWER to enter into alliances as equals.[65]

While an analysis of gender alone cannot provide the foundation for a strong women's movement for Jordan, the formal and semi-autonomous organization of women is vital to a revolutionary movement. Jordan and Robinson both support a theory of the political contingency of gender in struggle. In their analyses, since women do not carry commensurate political weight as men in unions or in Left parties because of their gender, they must begin to organize on the basis of their gender. When this organization develops, Jordan argues, Leftist women's organizational strength will translate into left coalitions working towards common goals.

Likewise, in early organizational theories of struggle, race as a category does not privilege one group of women's revolutionary potential over another's, but marks the structural determinants of their roles within and outside oppositional movements. The system of racism in the United States channels working-class women of color into more exploitative social and economic conditions than it does working-class white women. Jordan argues that because of the constitutive effects of systemic racism, black women need more than separate organization; they must lead the revolutionary women's movement. As Jordan states in the same letter:

> It seems to me that due to triple exploitation as workers, Negroes and women, that black women's organizations are probably best for your purposes at *this stage* of the struggle. But I think that black women are going to have to play a leadership role in women's organization generally (her emphasis).[66]

Again, Jordan qualifies the political and historical contingency of black women's organizations, given the conditions of political struggle. She emphasizes that because race and gender determine the character of class exploitation, being a woman of color in the American working class means triple exploitation; therefore; Black women must lead women's political struggle against their exploitation.[67]

Leadership questions within the movement were never divorced from the struggles those movements espoused, or the goals they fought to achieve. Policies and structures within political organization did not seek to harness struggle so much as to enable the possibilities disparate struggles unearthed and actively produced. As such, the movement through organization also sought to lead a wider range of political struggles. Robinson and Jordan never published their theories of organization, though they did distribute their letters to other activists. In this sense, these letters were public expressions of organizational theory among political organizers. They did not seek, on the basis of their writings, to lead the progressive women's movement or the Left more generally. Though it was never explicitly stated, passing the letters among organizers suggests that their intent may have been to lead through practice and through the example of the success of their methods of organization.

Feminism today has lost the nuanced quality of political analysis these documents reveal. The documents raise concerns about interconnection, political values, long-term goals, leadership, and representation in political movements that we still need to debate for our present context. The answers cannot remain the same

as those expressed by Weathers, Jordan, Benston, or Robinson, but their methodological insights still provide inspiration to continue the discussion. They suggest
explicitly organizational counterarguments to postfoundationalist support for autonomy and semi-autonomy in the proliferation of struggles. Where Butler sees ongoing self-differentiation as dynamic feminist practice, Weathers sees a means to an
end. Autonomy of struggles, like the autonomy of movements, can revitalize rigid
structures of leadership and the primacy of particular political formations. These
struggles can derail existing mechanisms of resources and expectations for who and
what should lead. But autonomy is not, for Weathers, glorified ahistorically as a political stance. Jordan and Robinson suggest that leadership by groups and ideas does
not determine the movement—in fact, as in the case of Women in Action—political
struggle often leads and operates independently of leadership forces in a movement.
At a more abstract level, they suggest that the feminist intellectual cannot begin to
understand organization separate from organized and unorganized struggle.

Ebert's theory of a self-critical feminism provides another framework to understand Robinson's and Jordan's letters about the women's movement. Robinson
and Jordan contest the values of an emerging women's movement, one that seeks
leaders of the movement over the struggles that loosely compose that movement.
Their writings were largely collective efforts, with authorship accredited to
Women in Action or Mothers Alone Working. Yet these documents' collective authorship does not obviate the need for more comprehensive or individually authored
writing. Neither do these articles denounce highly theoretical formulations. What
Robinson and others call for is a practice of writing that significantly reflects the
worth of often local and incremental struggles in the larger movement. They demand an intellectual engagement that takes seriously the ideas learned from activism, even when these ideas are written in informal venues, and spoken about in
plain language. Their disgust with Benston's methods and the gaps in her article is
not just a desire for credit, but is disgust with a product that fails to takes its own
production into account. Robinson and Jordan illustrate a self-critical stance in
Ebert's terms. They point to another set of intellectual practices, one that scholars
such as Benston should follow, even when writing for Leftist academic journals: self-
critical intellectual praxis, in the tradition of Robinson, Jordan, and Ebert, embeds
the product and its production in the struggles and movement it seeks to com-
municate.

CONCLUSION

The memory-work in this book does not aspire to provide a more objective view of what happened in U.S. feminism. Precisely because its focus is not on assessing the truth or the great meaning of disparate and usually ephemeral texts, memory-work is not a methodology for nostalgia, though idiosyncratic in similar ways. Memory-work helps to assess the activist past of the second wave women's movement amidst a flurry of books deeply invested in the same project. These memoirs, collections of ephemeral essays, biographies, and autobiographies, particularly, piece together the past to provide tools for the future. In this book, I focus on texts that were meant to be read by more than one person; even the letters were often copied and sent by the receiver to other friends, activists, and groups or sent en masse by the writer herself. Memory-work, like nostalgia, relies on value to produce meaning and interpretation. But nostalgia reconstructs the past; memory-work imagines new sets of beginnings.

I stress those potentialities, those paths that opened briefly in pockets around the country but were discarded. Rosalyn Baxandall and Linda Gordon argue that our histories of the women's movement have produced and reproduced serious gaps in the fabric of second wave feminism.[1] Certain groups, particularly those in New York, dominate the landscape, while innovations in the Midwest are largely ignored. Likewise, certain campaigns and tactics that competed with many other experiments gain a posthumous dominance, while others disappear without eliciting a murmur. Socialist feminism and radical feminism, they argue, have disappeared from our definitions of feminism.[2] To remember the past, then, requires a certain dismembering of present historical memories to retrieve lessons left out. I suggest a task more overtly political: that we reassess these pasts in the context of *our* politics, as much as in their original locations. Memory-work, by necessity, derives its value through the present dilemmas we face in struggle.

In most of these chapters I begin my excavation through present debates in feminism. Long-standing and often acrimonious disagreement give obvious clues as to what feminists consider important, but also point toward questions that haven't gained collective resolution over time and experience. Dissent in politics, particularly intramovement dissent, contains the potential for better methods and more responsive answers. Inderpal Grewal and Caren Kaplan comment on the questionable retreat to postfeminism as a resolution for conflicts too challenging for many feminists to face:

> We believe that many white, bourgeois feminists have announced a postfeminist era precisely because their particular definitions of feminism (which often require universalization) have not been able to withstand critiques from women of color as well as the deconstructions of poststructuralist or postmodern theory.[3]

If postfeminism clears the field of disturbing possibilities, the impulse behind this abdication can also cede ground to innovators. Feminist activism in the United States today may not have the breadth of a concentrated movement behind it, but the projects that led and follow critiques of feminism forge new movements and formations.

My theoretical guides for sorting through the campaigns of early second wave feminism have these utilitarian ends in mind. Organization, originally conceived by architects of early-twentieth-century communism to tailor statist daily politics to internationalist ambitions, undergoes a radical rewriting to measure post-Fordist political responses to the consolidation of multinational capitalism. In this book, organization meets its more flexible and high-profile ally, struggle, in very different combinations. Organization often drops from view precisely as it begins to integrate gains won by numerous, disaggregate struggles. It cannot, however, pull together into a continuous, progressive narrative how a movement in general, and the second wave women's movement in the United States in particular, envisions achievement. While struggle holds romantic possibilities of lightning-quick reflexes and locally customized methods, its romanticism hides a pragmatic compromise. In the present context, loosely interrelated struggles are random, and therefore more able to defend against crushing retaliation than to realize an inspired offense. Organization takes the next step and dares to imagine a future strength built from these often piecemeal efforts.

In this book, I create the rudiments of organization through an evaluation of the tools in second wave feminist struggles. Coalition, alliance, and affinity, as much as issues, operate through the structure of groups. Organization, as I conceive it, allows me to uncover how assumptions about a formation, about membership, and about political subjects create movement. As the site where theory meets practice, organization is less about a fixed plan for action than a site for possibility and creativity. These chapters do not address the details of specific campaigns, from either the past or the present. Instead, I attempt to lay the groundwork for how we can begin to think about the challenges we face in our localities and in our more visionary intentions.

NOTES

INTRODUCTION

1. Consolidation of its present legacy must do battle against, as one book's title proclaims, encroaching "feminist amnesia." Jean Curthoys, *Feminist Amnesia: The Wake of Women's Liberation* (London and: Routledge, 1997).

2. Karla Jay, *Tales of the Lavender Menace: A Memoir of Liberation* (New York: Basic Books, 1999); Susan Brownmiller, *In Our Time: Memoir of a Revolution* (New York: Dial Press, 1999).

3. Daniel Horowitz, *Betty Friedan and the Making of the Feminine Mystique: The American Left, the Cold War, and Modern Feminism* (Amherst: University of Massachusetts Press, 1998); Christine Wallace, *Germaine Greer: Untamed Shrew* (New York: Faber and Faber, 1998).

4. Rachel Blau DuPlessis and Ann Snitow, *The Feminist Memoir Project: Voices from Women's Liberation* (New York: Three Rivers Press, 1998).

5. Barbara Crow, ed., *Radical Feminism: A Documentary Reader* (New York: New York University Press, 2000); Alma M. Garcia, ed., *Chicana Feminist Thought: The Basic Historical Writings* (New York: Routledge, 1997); Ruth Rosen, *The World Split Open: How the Modern Women's Movement Changed America* (New York: Viking Press, 2000); Sheila Tobias, *Faces of Feminism: An Activist's Reflections on the Women's Movement* (Boulder: Westview Press, 1997). In addition, a 1999 reprint makes Flora Davis's history available again. Davis, *Moving the Mountain: The Women's Movement in America since 1960* (1991; reprint, Urbana: University of Illinois Press, 1991).

6. Many of these texts are explicitly framed in relation to the second women's movement; see Barbara Findlen, ed., *Listen Up: Voices from the Next Feminist Generation* (Seattle: Seal Press, 1995).

7. Many of these recent books end with an appeal to feminisms and feminists of the future. For example, see Nancy Whittier's *Feminist Generations: The Persistence of the Radical Women's Movement* (Philadelphia: Temple University Press, 1995).

8. Frigga Haug, *Female Sexualization: A Collective Work of Memory* (London: Verso, 1999).

9. Ibid., 35.

10. Rosen, *World Split Open*, xv.

11. Brownmiller, *In Our Time*, 10.

12. Haug, *Female Sexualization*, 41.

13. Jay, *Lavender Menace*, 2.

14. For a collection of excellent methodological essays on this problem, see Heidi Gottfried, ed., *Feminism and Social Change: Bridging Theory and Practice* (Urbana: University of Illinois Press, 1996).

15. Katie King takes a similar approach in her wide-ranging book about the issues faced by the U.S. women's movements. She takes polemic activist and measured academic articles equally seriously as documents of feminist thought. Katie King, *Theory in Its Feminist Travels: Conversations in U.S Women's Movements* (Bloomington: Indiana University Press, 1994.)

16. Lisa Duggan and Nan D. Hunter, *Sex Wars: Sexual Dissent and Political Culture* (New York: Routledge, 1995); Lisa Duggan, "Theory Wars, or Who's Afraid of Judith Butler?" *Journal of Women's History* 10:1 (Spring 1998): 9–20; Shane Phelan, *Identity Politics: Lesbian Feminism and the Limits of Community* (Philadelphia: Temple University Press, 1989); Shane Phelan, *Getting Specific: Post Modern Lesbian Politics* (Minneapolis: University of Minnesota Press, 1995).

17. Another welcome approach addresses feminist influences in politics that may not be labeled "feminist" or identified solely as part of a women's movement. See Robin Teske, ed., *Conscious Acts and the Politics of Social Change* (Columbia: University of South Carolina Press, 2000); Jill M. Bystydzienski and Joti Sekhon, eds., *Democratization and Women's Grassroots Movements* (Bloomington: Indiana University Press, 1999).

18. Nancy Fraser, *Justice Interruptus: Critical Reflections on the 'Postsocialist' Condition* (New York: Routledge, 1997).

19. For one recent and very challenging example of imagining feminism with a larger social vision, see Teresa Ebert, *Ludic Feminism and After* (Ann Arbor: University of Michigan Press, 1996).

20. This emphasis on the collective political subject attempts to reframe significantly Melucci's limited, though not wholly inaccurate, definition of the "new" character of New Social Movements, a school that usually includes the women's movement after 1967 in its purview. Melucci defines second wave feminism, among other movements, as distinguished by "the quest for self that addresses the fundamental regions of human action: the body, the emotions, the dimensions of experience irreducible to instrumental rationality." Alberto Melucci, "A Strange Kind of Newness: What's New in New Social Movements?" in *New Social Movements: From Ideology to Identity*, ed. Enrique Larana, Hank Johnston and Joseph R. Gusfield (Philadelphia: Temple University Press, 1994), 112.

21. Joy James centers her study of class and gender in African-American politics around the question of leadership. Her insightful book addresses with historical breadth and sensitivity issues of consensus, representation, and leadership as they developed in the twentieth century. In particular, see "The Common Program: Race, Class, Sex and Politics," in *Transcending the Talented Tenth: Black Leaders and American Intellectuals* (New York: Routledge, 1997).

22. Joreen, "The Tyranny of Structurelessness," *in Radical Feminism*, ed. Anne Koedt, Ellen Levine, and Anita Rapone (New York: Quadrangle Books, 1974), 285–99.

23. Donna Haraway, "A Cyborg Manifesto: Science, Technology, and Socialist-Feminism in the Late Twentieth Century," in *Simians, Cyborgs, and Women* (New York: Routledge, 1991).

24. Amanda Anderson cogently outlines a similar quality in Judith Butler's post-foundationalist politics; see her essay "Debatable Performances: Restaging Contentious Feminisms," Social Text, 16:1 (Spring 1998): 1–24.

25. For a compelling argument about the limitation of poststructuralist theories for politics see Paula M. L. Moya, "Chicana Feminism and Postmodernist Theory", Signs 26:2 (Winter 2001): 441–484.

26. See, for example, Alice Echols's description of politicos versus feminists in chapters 2 and 3 of her history of radical feminism, Daring to Be Bad: Radical Feminism in America, 1967–1975 (Minneapolis: University of Minnesota Press, 1987); Barbara Ryan, Feminism and the Women's Movement (New York: Routledge, 1992), 46–48; Roberta Salper, "The Development of the Women's Liberation Movement, 1967–1971," in Female Liberation: History and Current Politics, ed. Roberta Salper (New York: Alfred A. Knopf, 1972), 169–84.

27. Ellen Rooney and Gayatri Spivak, "In a Word," in Outside in the Teaching Machine, Gayatri Spivak (New York: Routledge), 2.

28. Georg Lukács, "Towards a Methodology of the Problem of Organization," in History and Class Consciousness (Cambridge: MIT Press, 1971), 304.

29. Ann Snitow, "Pages from a Gender Diary," Dissent (Spring, 1989): 205–24.

30. Ibid., 205.

31. Rosa Luxemburg, The Mass Strike, The Political Party and the Trade Unions (London: Merlin Press, 1964). See in particular the chapter entitled "The Interaction of the Political and the Economic Struggle."

CHAPTER ONE

1. Ginia Bellafante, "Feminism: It's All About Me!" Time, 29 June 1998, 54–60.

2. From a telephone poll of 721 adult American women taken by TIME/CNN, May 18–19, by Yankelovich Partners Inc. They report that the percentage of American women who considered themselves feminists fell from 32 in 1989 to 25 in 1998 and the percentage of America in women who did not consider themselves feminists rose from 58 to 65, p. 58.

3. For an antidote to this representation, see Johanna Brenner, "The Best of Times; The Worst of Times: US Feminism Today," New Left Review 209 (1993): 101–159.

4. Barbara Findlen, ed., Listen up: Voices from the Next Feminist Generation (Seattle: Seal Press, 1995); Leslie Heywood and Jennifer Drake, eds., Feminist Agenda: Being Feminist, Doing Feminism (Minneapolis: University of Minnesota Press, 1997); Rebecca Walker, ed., To Be Real (New York: Anchor, 1995).

5. Catherine Orr, "Charting the currents of the third wave," Hypatia, 12:3 (1997): 29–45.

6. Edith Hoshino Altbach, ed., From Feminism to Liberation (Cambridge, MA: Schenkman, 1971); Toni Cade, ed., The Black Woman: An Anthology (New York: Signet Books, 1970); Robin Morgan, ed., Sisterhood is Powerful (New York: Vintage, 1970); Sookie Stambler, ed., Women's Liberation: Blueprint for the Future (New York: Ace Books, 1970); Leslie Tanner, ed., Voices from Women's Liberation (New York: Signet, 1971). A prominent exception is Cellestine Ware, Woman Power: The Movement for Women's Liberation (New York: Tower, 1970).

7. For a detailed discussion of the personal narratives in relation to organizational concerns, see Deborah L. Siegel, "The Legacy of the Personal: Generating Theory in Feminism's Third Wave," *Hypatia* 12:3 (1997): 46–75.

8. Walker, xxxiii–xxxiv.

9. V. I. Lenin, *What Is to Be Done?* (New York: International Publishers, 1969); Georg Lukács, "Towards a Methodology of the Problem of Organization," in *History and Class Consciousness* (Cambridge: MIT Press, 1986), 295–342; Rosa Luxemburg, *The Mass Strike, The Political Party and The Trade Unions* (London: Merlin Press, 1964).

10. In this chapter I discuss two professionally published essays in the most detail alongside more informal, less widely distributed publications. Margaret Benston, "The Political Economy of Women's Liberation," in *From Feminism to Liberation,* ed. Altbach, 199–210. The article was first published in *Monthly Review* (September 1969). Juliet Mitchell, "Women: The Longest Revolution," *New Left Review* 40 (1966): 11–37.

11. Alice Echols's history also records the importance of debates about class and race to early feminist formations. See Alice Echols, *Daring to Be Bad: Radical Feminism in America, 1967–1975* (Minneapolis: University of Minnesota Press, 1987), 105–9.

12. Other examples, though published some years after Mitchell's and Benston's articles, include a journal special issue: "The Political Economy of Women," *The Review of Radical Political Economics* 4:3 (July 1972); Marilyn Power Goldberg (Berkeley Women's Liberation), "The Economic Exploitation of Women," (n.d.), Women's Ephemera Files (WEF), Socioeconomic Theories—Papers, Folder 3 Northwestern University (NU), Chicago, IL. Barbara Bergmann, "The Economics of Women's Liberation" (paper for the American Psychological Association convention, September 1971), WEF, Socioeconomic Theories—Papers, Folder 3, NU, Chicago, IL.

13. Lukács, "Towards a Methodology," 299.

14. Daniel Horowitz, *Betty Friedan and the Making of "The Feminine Mystique:" The American Left, The Cold War, and Modern Feminism* (Amherst: University of Massachusetts Press, 1998).

15. Leila J. Rupp and Verta Taylor, *Survival in the Doldrums: The American Women's Rights Movement, 1945 to the 1960s* (London: Oxford University Press, 1987).

16. The complexity of Guy-Shefthall's volume counteracts more homogenized liberal genealogies of African-American feminism that Joy James argues mark the scholarly landscape. Beverly Guy-Shefthall, ed., *Words of Fire: An Anthology of African-American Feminist Thought* (New York: The New Press, 1995). James discusses the example of Patricia Hill Collins' influential book, *Black Feminist Thought.* Joy James, *Transcending the Talented Tenth: Black Leaders and American Intellectuals* (New York: Routledge, 1997), 94–97.

17. Katie King, *Theory in Its Feminist Travels: Conversations in U.S. Women's Movements* (Bloomington: Indiana University Press, 1994).

18. Ibid., 3.

19. Ibid., 21.

20. Rosemary Hennessy and Chrys Ingraham, eds., *Materialist Feminism: A Reader in Class, Difference, and Women's Lives* (New York: Routledge, 1997). See also Karen V. Hansen and Ilene J. Philipson, eds., *Women, Class, and the Feminist Imagination: A Socialist-Feminist Reader* (Philadelphia: Temple University Press, 1990).

21. Linda Nicholson ed., *The Second Wave: A Reader in Feminist Theory* (New York: Routledge, 1997).

22. Nancy Fraser, *Justice Interruptus: Critical Reflections on the "Postsocialist" Condition* (New York: Routledge, 1997). For another recent book that draws on this paradigm, see Judith Evans, *Feminist Theory Today: An Introduction to Second-Wave Feminism* (London: Sage Books, 1995).

23. For an early and very influential outline of gender and formal equality see Pauli Murray, "Jane Crow and the Law: Sex Discrimination and Title VII," *George Washington Law Review* 34:2 (December 1965): 232–56.

24. Betty Friedan positions her book, *The Feminine Mystique*, as an attack against biological arguments about women's natural inferiority to men. In the seventies and eighties arguments for women's equality were set against feminist theories of women's innate, albeit superior, differences from men, a position illustrated by Mary F. Belenkey, ed., *Women's Ways of Knowing* (New York: Harper Collins, 1997).

25. Tobias historicizes the rubric of "difference" with the publication in 1982 of Carol Gilligan's book *In a Different Voice,* 9. Sheila Tobias, *Faces of Feminism: An Activist's Reflections on the Women's Movement* (Boulder, CO: Westview Press, 1997).

26. Ann Snitow, "Pages from a Gender Diary," *Dissent* (1989): 205–24; Echols, *Daring to be Bad.*

27. Nancy Fraser admits that advocates of a wide range of politics, from liberal to radical to socialist, used the term *equality* in the early stages of the second wave women's movement. She argues, however, that they all subverted gender difference. We lose, in her characterization, the very definition of liberation in this period of the women's movement.

28. For a more thorough analysis of difference in relation to feminism, see Linda Gordon's critique, "On 'Difference,'" *Genders,* 10 (Spring 1991): 91–111.

29. For a related criticism about the unitary focus on the subject, see Teresa Ebert, "The 'Difference' of Postmodern Feminism," *College English,* 53:8 (December 1991): 886–904.

30. The schism between revolutionary and reformist politics has a much longer trajectory in U.S. feminism than just the debates in the sixties and seventies. For historical accounts of this debate, see Mari Jo Buhle, *Women and American Socialism, 1870–1920* (Urbana: University of Illinois Press, 1983) and Nancy F. Cott, *The Grounding of Modern Feminism* (New Haven: Yale University Press, 1987).

31. For another recent feminist theoretical engagement with political economy, see J. K. Gibson-Graham, *The End of Capitalism (As We Knew It): A Feminist Critique of Political Economy* (London: Blackwell, 1996).

32. The historical details and urgency of these debates have been well explored by a number of scholars; see Norman Geras, *The Legacy of Rosa Luxemburg* (New York: Schocken Books, 1976); Dick Howard, *Selected Political Writings of Rosa Luxemburg* (New York: Monthly Review Press, 1971); and Istvan Meszaros, *Lukács's Concept of Dialectic* (New York: Harper and Row, 1972).

33. In Britain, as in the United States, child care was seen as one important condition of possibility for women's participation in radical politics. Vicky Randall looks with careful attention to the social relations of these feminist politics and why even reformist campaigns like this one so often failed to yield political or material results. Vicky Randall, "Feminism and Child Daycare," *Journal of Social Policy,* 25:4 (October 1996): 485–506. For a contemporary example of this demand, see Dena Attar, "Is There Childcare for this Event?" *Connexions* 43 (Summer 1993): 22–25.

34. Revolutionary politics, depending on how they were defined, could just as easily force a complete split between the women's movement and other social movements.

35. An early form of this essay was first published in 1921; entitled "Organizational Problems of the Revolutionary Movement," it was printed in the magazine *The International*.

36. Lukács, "Towards a Methodology," 299.

37. Lenin, *What is to be Done?*

38. Lukács, "Towards a Methodology," 297.

39. Ibid., 300.

40. Ibid., 329–30.

41. Luxemburg, *The Mass Strike*, 35.

42. Ibid., 62.

43. Marlene Dixon, "Where are We Going?" in *From Feminism to Liberation*, ed. Altbach 53–63.

44. For a detailed description of the conference see Echols, *Daring to Be Bad*, 108-14.

45. Dixion,"Where Are We Going?" 550.

46. Simone De Beauvoir, *The Second Sex* (New York: Knopf, 1952).

47. Mitchell's argument is not as exceptional as it seems in a history of second wave feminism. Two years after De Beauvoir's book was translated into English (1952) the National Women's Commission of the Communist Party USA published an analysis markedly similar to Mitchell's. National Women's Commission, Communist Party USA, "Some Notes on Simone De Beauvoir's Book, *Woman: The Second Sex*," Joan Jordan Papers, Box 1, Wisconsin State Historical Society (WSHS), Madison, WI.

48. Mitchell, "Women: The Longest Revolution," 18.

49. Ibid., 17.

50. Sara Evans, *Personal Politics: The Roots of Women's Liberation in the Civil Rights Movement and the New Left* (New York: Knopf, 1979).

51. Clara Fraser, "The Emancipation of Women" (Radical Women Publications), Melba Windoffer Papers, Acc. 1798-2, Box 3, Manuscripts and University Archives, University of Washington, Seattle, WA. The article was first published in the Freedom Socialist Party's journal *Revolutionary Age* 1:3 (1968).

52. Mary King, *Freedom Song: A Personal Story of the 1960s Civil Rights Movement* (New York: Morrow, 1987), appendix.

53. Clara Fraser, "The Emancipation of Women," 4.

54. Joan Jordan, "The Place of American Women: Economic Exploitation of Women," WEF, Socioeconomic Theories—Papers, Folder 3, NU, Chicago, IL. The essay was first published in *Revolutionary Age* 1:3 (1968).

55. Benston, "Political Economy of Women's Liberation," 200.

56. Ibid., 201.

57. Shulamith Firestone, *The Dialectic of Sex: The Case for Feminist Revolution* (New York: Quill, William Morrow, 1970).

58. Firestone, Ibid., 12.

59. Benston, "Political Economy of Women's Liberation," 209.

60. Joreen, "What in the Hell Is Women's Liberation Anyway?" *Voice of the Women's Liberation Movement* 1:1 (March 1968): 1, 4.

61. Benston, "Political Economy of Women's Liberation," 202; Firestone, *Dialectic of Sex,* 19.

62. Dixon, "Where Are We Going?" 62.

63. Wednesday Nite Group, Berkeley Women's Liberation, "The Nature of Change and Political Action—Reform vs. Revolution" (n.d.), WEF, Socioeconomic Theories—Papers, Folder 6, NU, Chicago, IL.

64. Many position papers on day care and reproductive rights drew on a similar understanding of reform in a revolutionary movement. See for example, "Third World Proposal on Reproductive Rights," (1971) Women's Liberation Files, Niebyl Proctor Marxist Library for Social Research, Berkeley, CA; "Politics of Day Care" (n.d.), WEF, Child Care-Position Papers, NU, Chicago, IL; Lisa Leghorn (Female Liberation, Boston), "Child Care for the Child," WEF, Child Care-Position Papers, NU, Chicago, IL.

65. Kathy McAfee and Myrna Wood, "Bread and Roses," in *From Feminism to Liberation,* ed. Altbach, 36. The essay was first published in *Leviathan* 1:3 (June 1969): 8–11, 43–44.

66. Firestone, *Dialectic of Sex,* 20.

67. Ibid., 44.

CHAPTER TWO

1. Rebecca Walker, ed., *To Be Real* (New York: Anchor, 1995).

2. Often this contentious process is simplified to a narrative of progress from (white) feminism's ethnocentrism (dating from 1970 to 1985) to their subsequent awareness. For example, see Elizabeth Abel's essay "Black Writing, White Reading: Race and the Politics of Feminist Interpretation," *in Female Subjects in Black and White: Race, Psychoanalysis, Feminism,* ed. Elizabeth Abel, Barbara Christian, and Helene Moglen (Berkeley: University of California Press, 1997), 106–7.

3. Linda Alcoff, "Cultural Feminism Versus Post-Structuralism: The Identity Crisis in Feminist Theory," *Signs* 13:3 (1988): 405–36; Deborah McDowell, "Transferences: Black Feminist Thinking: The 'Practice' of 'Theory'" in *"The Changing Same": Black Women's Literature, Criticism and Theory* (Bloomington: Indiana University Press, 1995), 156–75.

4. Alcoff, "Cultural Feminism," 405.

5. McDowell, "Transferences," 160.

6. Adrienne Rich, "Disobedience is What NWSA is Potentially About," *Women's Studies Quarterly* 9:3 (Fall 1981): 4.

7. Catherine R. Stimpson, "A Critical View of Women's Studies," *Women's Studies Newsletter* 2 (1972): 1–4.

8. NWSA, "From the Steering Committee," *Women's Studies Newsletter* 8:2 (1980): 13.

9. Ellen Rooney, *Seductive Reasoning: Pluralism in Literary Theory* (Ithaca: Cornell University Press, 1989), 12–13.

10. Stacey Young argues that the radical demands of antiracist feminism have been reinterpreted and understood through the dominant paradigm of liberal pluralism, to the detriment of these demands (Stacey Young, *Changing the Wor(l)d: Discourse, Politics and the Feminist Movement* (New York: Routledge, 1997).

11. Rooney, *Seductive Reasoning*, 3.

12. Maxine Baca Zinn, Lynn Weber Cannon, Elizabeth Higginbotham, and Bonnie Thornton Dill, "The Costs of Exclusionary Practices in Women's Studies," *Signs* 11:2 (1986): 290–303.

13. Rayna Reiter, ed., *Toward an Anthropology of Women* (New York: Monthly Review Press, 1975); Berenice A. Carroll, ed., *Liberating Women's History: Theoretical and Critical Essays* (Urbana: University of Illinois Press, 1976); Ann D. Gordon, Mari Jo Buhle, and Nancy Schrom Dye, *Women in American Society* (Somerville, MA: New England Free Press, n.d.).

14. Elizabeth V. Spelman, *Inessential Woman: Problems of Exclusion in Feminist Thought* (Boston: Beacon Press, 1988), 115.

15. "About the National Women's Studies Association," *Frontiers* 5:1 (1980): 1.

16. Barbara Smith, "Racism and Women's Studies," in *Making Face, Making Soul, Haciendo Caras,* ed. Gloria Anzaldua (San Francisco: Aunt Lute Books, 1990), 25.

17. Patricia Frech and Barbara Hillyer Davis, "The NWSA Constituency: Evaluation of the 1979 Conference Participation," *Frontiers* 5:1 (1980): 68.

18. Stimpson, "A Critical View," 1–4.

19. Marilyn Boxer, "For and About Women: The Theory and Practice of Women's Studies in the United States," *Signs* 7:3 (Spring 1982): 678–79.

20. Norma J. Cobbs and Pat Miller, "NWSA Convention '81: Women and Racism," *Women's Studies Newsletter* 8:3 (Summer 1980): 26.

21. See Joan Scott's keynote address, which focuses on the combined threats of antifeminism, Reaganism, and the sexism of the academy, "Politics and Professionalism: Women Historians in the 1980s," *Women's Studies Quarterly* 9:3 (Fall 1981): 23–31. Florence Howe, a commanding presence in the formation of women's studies, notes with dismay the heightened pressure on NWSA, a pressure absent in conferences such as the Berkshire conference; see her editorial in the same issue of *Women's Studies Quarterly,* p. 2.

22. Deborah Rosenfelt, "A Time for Confrontation," *Women's Studies Quarterly* 9:3 (Fall 1981): 11.

23. For an the overview of consciousness-raising sessions, see *Women's Studies Quarterly* 9:3 (Fall 1981): 13–16.

24. Nancy Polikoff, "Addressing Racism," *Off Our Backs* 10:7 (1980): 19.

25. Elizabeth Schultz and Janet Sharistanian, "Some Thoughts on the Integration of Diversity," *Women's Studies Newsletter* 7:3 (Summer 1979): 5.

26. Stimpson, "A Critical View," 1980, 5–6.

27. Rich, "Disobedience," 6.

28. Audre Lorde, "Uses of Anger," *Sister Outsider* (Freedom, CA: Crossing Press, 1984), 131.

29. Peggy Way, Joan Brown, and Helen Fannings, "Liberation's Struggle Generates Tension on Race, Sex Issues," *The Christian Century* (10 June 1970). Social Action Vertical File, Box 58, Wisconsin State Historical Society (WSHS), Madison, WI.

30. Alice Echols' history of radical feminism, *Daring to be Bad,* discusses the planning meetings for one of the first national meetings of the women's liberation movement, which touched on the participation of black women in the predominantly white WLM. She portrays, with disturbing sympathy, the dominant argument that WLM should remain a white women's movement, in part due to the white women's discomfort with black activist women. See Alice Echols, *Daring to be Bad: Radical Feminism in America, 1967–1975* (Minneapolis: University of Minnesota Press, 1989) 104–7, appendix A.

31. One example from the Left stresses the need to "broaden the base of our movement by talking to working-class black and white women . . . and show in practice that 'women's liberation' is not a white thing, but a revolutionary thing." See Terry Radinsky and Lucy Gadlin, "Towards a Revolutionary Women's Union: A Strategic Perspective" (xerox leaflet), WEF, Socio-economic Theories—Papers, Folder 7, NU, Chicago, IL.

32. See Robin Morgan's introduction to her edited volume *Sisterhood is Powerful,* which characterizes black women's participation in feminism as the slow but hopeful growth of black women's groups in the black liberation movement and their "perfectly organic" relationship to the larger WLM. Robin Morgan, ed., *Sisterhood is Powerful* (New York: Vintage Books, 1970), xxvi.

33. Louis Harris and Associates, Inc., "The 1972 Virginia Slims American Women's Opinion Poll: A Survey of Attitudes of Women on their Roles in Politics and the Economy," cited in Maren Lockwood Carden, *The New Feminist Movement* (New York: Russell Sage Foundation, 1974), 29.

34. Probably the most common reason given in the late sixties and early seventies, by black and white women, was that black women needed to secure black liberation before fighting for women's liberation (or racism trumps sexism). See Edith Hoshino Altbach, "Introduction: Notes on a Movement," in *From Feminism to Liberation,* ed., Edith Hoshino Altbach (Cambridge: Schenkman, 1971), 9. For a range of positions by politically active black women within and outside the women's movement, see Betty Jean Overton, "Black Women in Women's Liberation," *Race Relations Reporter* (1 July 1970), Black Women File, Schlesinger Library, Radcliffe College, Cambridge.

35. Mirta Vidal, "Women: New Voice of La Raza," *Chicanas Speak Out* (New York: Pathfinder Press, 1971), 3–11; for later articles about the women's movement in relation to Native American, Latina, and Asian American women, see *Civil Rights Digest* 6:3 (1974).

36. One untitled, undated flyer from the late sixties or early seventies that speaks for Gay Women's Liberation in the Bay Area bluntly states, "Women's Liberation and Gay Women's Liberation, we feel, has never properly dealt with its own racism—as witness to the fact that there are only a few black women or third world women in women's liberation and gay women's liberation." Vertical Files, Women's Liberation Movement, Center for Socialist History, Berkeley, CA.

37. Frances Beale, "Double Jeopardy: To Be Black and Female," in *Words of Fire,* ed., Beverly Guy-Sheftall (New York: The New Press, 1995), 153. Guy-Sheftall mistakenly locates the article's first publication in Morgan's *Sisterhood is Powerful* (1970); the article was published earlier in *Motive* (March–April 1969).

38. See also articles by Maryanne Weathers, "An Argument for Black Women's Liberation as a Revolutionary Force," in *Words of Fire,* ed. Guy-Shefthall (1968); and Maxine Williams, "Why Women's Liberation is Important to Black Women," in *Black Women's Liberation* ed., Maxine Williams and Pamela Newman (New York: Pathfinder Press, 1970).

39. Linda La Rue, "The Black Movement and Women's Liberation," *The Black Scholar* (1970): 2–8.

40. Ibid., 7.

41. For example, see books by historians about feminism and unions as well as about unrecognized forms of feminism after World War II, respectively: Diane Balser, *Sisterhood and Solidarity* (Boston: South End Press, 1987); Leila J. Rupp and Verta Taylor, *Survival in the Doldrums: The American Women's Rights Movement, 1945 to the 1960s* (Oxford: Oxford University Press, 1987).

CHAPTER THREE

1. Carol Biewener, "A Postmodern Encounter: Post-Structuralist Feminism and the Decentering of Marxism," *Socialist Review* 27:1–2 (Winter-Spring 1999): 71–97; Seyla Benhabib, "Feminism and Postmodernism," in *Feminist Contentions: A Philosophical Exchange* (New York: Routledge, 1995), 17–34; Barbara Ehrenreich and Janet McIntosh, "The New Creationism," *The Nation,* 264:22 (June 9, 1997): 11–16; Barbara Epstein, "Postmodernism and the Left," *New Politics,* 6:2 (Winter 1997).

2. Linda Alcoff, "Cultural Feminism Versus Post-Structuralism: The Identity Crisis in Feminist Theory," *Signs* 13:3 (1988): 405–36.

3. Butler most thoroughly develops her ideas about performativity as a mode of politics in *Bodies That Matter.* This chapter focuses on her earlier book, *Gender Trouble,* and a later essay as they discuss more collective aspects of discursivity and politics. An essay by Pheng Cheah provides an insightful account of how Butler's ideas about performativity inform a kind of negative agency for bodies. Judith Butler, *Bodies That Matter: On the Discursive Limits of "Sex"* (New York: Routledge, 1993); Butler, *Gender Trouble* (New York: Routledge, 1990); Pheng Cheah, "Mattering," *Diacritics* 26:1 (Spring 1996): 108–39; Donna Haraway, *Simians, Cyborgs, and Women: The Reinvention of Nature* (New York: Routledge, 1991).

4. See Wini Breines, *Community and Organization in the New Left, 1962–1968* (New Brunswick: Rutgers University Press, 1989).

5. Sara Evans, *Personal Politics: The Roots of Women's Liberation in the Civil Rights Movement and the New Left* (New York: Knopf, 1979), 214–16; Maren Lockwood Carden, *The New Feminist Movement* (New York: Russell Sage Foundation, 1974), 19–30.

6. Gayatri Spivak, *In Other Worlds* (New York: Routledge, 1987).

7. Teresa de Lauretis, "Eccentric Subjects: Feminist Theory and Historical Consciousness," *Feminist Studies* 16:1 (Spring 1990): 115–50; Rosemary Hennessey, *Materialist Feminism and the Politics of Discourse* (New York: Routledge, 1993).

8. Hennessey, *Materialist Feminism,* xii.

9. Norma Alarcon, even as she recognizes the project of postmodern feminist theories to deconstruct a universal subject of feminism, asks, "[D]o they free women of color from the 'service of violence against themselves,' or do they rationalize it as well?" Norma Alarcon, "Traddutora, Traditora," in *Scattered Hegemonies,* ed. Inderpal Grewal and Caren Kaplan (Minneapolis: University of Minnesota Press, 1994), 130.

10. Judith Butler, "Contingent Foundations," in *Feminist Contentions,* eds. Scyla Bonhabib, Judith Butler, Drucilla Cornell, Nancy Fraser (New York: Rutledge, 1995), 50.

11. Judith Hole and Ellen Levine, *Rebirth of Feminism* (New York: Quadrangle Books, 1971), 108–66.

12. Alice Echols, *Daring to Be Bad: Radical Feminism in America, 1967–1975* (Minneapolis: University of Minnesota Press, 1987), 17.

13. Cheah stresses that for Butler this resistance is always within hegemonic discursive realms; there is no position for agency beyond or outside of those relations. Cheah, "Mattering," 118.

14. Butler, *Bodies That Matter,* 55.

15. Cheah, "Mattering," 121.

16. Butler, *Gender Trouble,* 16.

17. Butler, Ibid., 17.

18. Jennifer Wicke criticizes what she calls a lack of positionality in the postfoundationalist collection of essays *Feminists Theorize the Political.* Jennifer Wicke, "Celebrity Feminism," *South Atlantic Quarterly* 93:4 (1994): 769–70. For a similar assessment of postfoundationalist weaknesses, see Eleni Varikas, "Gender, Experience and Subjectivity: The Tilly-Scott Disagreement," *New Left Review* 211 (1995): 97.

19. Amanda Anderson, "Cryptonormativism and Double Gestures: The Politics of Post-Structuralism," *Cultural Critique* 21 (Spring 1992): 79.

20. Spivak, *In Other Worlds.*

21. Denise Riley, *Am I That Name? Feminism and the Category "Women" in History* (Minneapolis: University of Minnesota Press, 1988), 111.

22. See also, Chela Sandoval, "U.S. Third World Feminism: The Theory and Method of Oppositional Consciousness in the Postmodern World," *Genders* 10 (1991): 1–24.

23. Spivak, *In Other Worlds,* 205.

24. Later, in an interview with Ellen Rooney, Spivak stresses the importance of the word *strategic,* which she argues must apply to collective politics, not to validate one's reading over another's. See Ellen Rooney and Gayatri Spivak, "In a Word," *Outside the Teaching Machine* (New York: Routledge, 1993), 5.

25. Haraway, *Simians, Cyborgs and Women,* 149–81.

26. Ibid., 154–55.

27. Ibid., 155.

28. Ibid., 173.

29. Butler, *Gender Trouble,* 15.

30. Neil Lazarus, Steven Evans, Anthony Arnove, and Anne Menke, "The Necessity of Universalism," *differences* 7:1 (1995): 71–75.

31. Jenny Bourne, "Homelands of the Mind: Jewish Feminism and Identity Politics," *Race and Class* 24 (1987): 1–23; Diana Fuss, *Essentially Speaking* (New York: Routledge, 1989).

32. For more detailed accounts about the rise of the consciousness-raising group in second wave feminism, see Hole and Levine, *Rebirth of Feminism,* 108–66; Jo Freeman, *The Politics of Women's Liberation* (New York: David McKay, 1975), 103–46.

33. Bourne, "Homelands," 2.

34. Fuss, *Essentially Speaking,* 101.

35. Ibid., 100.

36. Spivak, "In a Word," 3.

37. Fuss, *Essentially Speaking*, 101.

38. Bourne, "Homelands," 2–3.

39. Marlene Dixon, "Public Ideology and the Class Composition of Women's Liberation (1966–1969)," *Berkeley Journal of Sociology* 16 (1971): 152.

40. Alice Echols describes one turning point for many feminists after the supposedly inclusive National Conference for New Politics harassed feminist delegates from raising the issue of sexism in the meeting, or admitting a conference resolution condemning sexism. See Echols, *Daring to Be Bad*, 45–50. Sara Evans's and Wini Breines's histories locate other similar turning points (of intragroup disenfranchisement) for women emerging from the student left and civil rights movements.

41. Marge Piercy. "Grand Coolie Dam," *Leviathan* 6 (November 1969): 22.

42. Bourne, "Homelands," 22. In this passage, she cites Franz Fanon's *Black Skin, White Masks* (New York: Grove Press, 1967).

43. Fuss, *Essentially Speaking*, 101.

44. Ibid., 101.

45. Ibid., 105.

46. Evans, *Personal Politics*, 214–15.

47. Freeman, *Politics of Women's Liberation*, 125–29.

48. See Judith Hole's and Ellen Levine's breakdown of women's liberation groups in New York from 1969 to 1970 for a sense of the diversity among loosely affiliated groups. Judith Hole and Ellen Levine, *Rebirth of Feminism* (New York: Quadrangle Books, 1971), 135–57.

49. Roberta Salper describes how these different positions figured women's liberation groups in the late sixties and early seventies. Roberta Salper, "The Development of the American Women's Liberation Movement, 1967–1971," in *Female Liberation*, ed. Roberta Salper (New York: Knopf, 1972), 169–84.

50. Freeman, *Politics of Women's Liberation*, 143.

51. Shulamith Firestone, *The Dialectic of Sex: The Case for Feminist Revolution* (New York: Quill, 1970), 44.

52. For early essays about participatory democracy within SDS see Mitchell Cohen and Dennis Hale, eds., *The New Student Left Anthology* (Boston: Beacon Press, 1966). Sara Evans makes a strong case for the centrality of student organizing models (used in the North and the South) to the emergence of the women's liberation movement.

53. For a detailed discussion of the tenets of participatory democracy, see James Forman, *The Making of Black Revolutionaries* (Washington, D.C.: Open Hand Publishing, 1985).

54. Elinor Langer, "Notes for the Next Time: A Memoir of the 1960s," *Working Papers for a New Society* 1 (Fall 1973): 48–83.

55. Ibid., 82–83.

56. Beverly Jones and Judith Brown, "Toward a Female Liberation Movement" (Gainesville, FL, 1968), 20, Social Action Vertical File, Box 58, WSHS, Madison, WI.

57. Ibid.

58. Pam Allen, "Free Space: A Perspective on the Small Group in Women's Liberation" (1968), Pam Allen Papers, Box 2, WSHS, Madison, WI.

59. Ibid, 33.

60. Pam Allen, "A Proposal for Women's Liberation to Begin to Develop Action Organizations" (n.d.),Women's Liberation Movement Vertical File, Center for Socialist History, Berkeley, CA.

61. Meredith Tax, "Working Paper: The Need for a Program, Strategy, and Political Organization in the Boston Women's Movement" (30 June 1969), Social Action Vertical File, Box 58, WSHS, Madison, WI.

62. New York Radical Feminists, "Organizing Principles of the New York Radical Feminists," *Notes for the Second Year* (1970): 120.

63. Ibid., 119.

64. Echols, *Daring to Be Bad,* 189.

65. Ellen Willis, "Women and the Left," *Notes from the Second Year—Major Writings of the Radical Feminists* (April 1970): 55.

66. Kathie Sarachild, "A Program for Feminist 'Consciousness Raising,'" *Notes from the Second Year—Major Writings of the Radical Feminists* (April 1970): 78–79.

67. Jones and Brown, *"Toward A Female Liberation Movement,"* 21.

68. Ibid., 31.

69. Joreen (Jo Freeman), "The Tyranny of Structurelessness," in *Radical Feminism,* ed. Anne Koedt, Ellen Levine, and Anita Rapone (New York: Quadrangle Books, 1974), 286–67.

70. Jennifer Gardiner, "The Small Group: The Prison Guards at Work," *The Woman's Page* 4 (18 February 1971): 7, cited in Echols, *Daring to Be Bad,* 155.

71. In her memoirs of the women's movement, Leah Fritz answers this question in the affirmative, since Onassis also faced sexual objectification. In Fritz's words, "The celebrity of her two husbands had made her an object of sexual wonder." See Leah Fritz, *Dreamers and Dealers: An Intimate Appraisal of the Women's Movement* (Boston: Beacon Press, 1979), 220. A variation on this question about universal sisterhood was answered by Dorothy Pitman in an interview in *Mademoiselle,* entitled "'I Can't Call You Sister Yet': A Black Woman Looks at Women's Lib," (May 1971): 182–83, 219–21.

72. Evans, *Personal Politics,* 214–15; Barbara Ryan, *Feminism and the Women's Movement* (New York: Routledge, 1992), 47. Katie King stresses the importance of consciousness-raising groups to theory building in *Theory in Its Feminist Travels: Conversations in U.S. Women's Movement,* (Bloomington: Indiana University Press, 1994), 127–28.

73. Uma Narayan, *Dislocating Culture: Identities, Traditions and Third World Feminism* (New York: Routledge, 1997).

74. Audre Lorde, "Uses of Anger," *Sister Outsider* (Freedom, CA: Crossing Press, 1984); Deborah McDowell, "Transferences: Black Feminist Thinking: The 'Practice' of 'Theory'" in *"The Changing Same": Black Women's Literature, Criticism and Theory* (Bloomington: Indiana University Press, 1995); Adrienne Rich, "Disobedience is What NWSA is Potentially About," *Women's Studies Quarterly* 9:3 (Fall 1981): 6.

75. Butler, *Gender Trouble,* 4.

76. Ibid, 5.

77. Ibid.

78. Haraway, *Simians, Cyborgs, and Women,* 163.

79. Ibid., 155.

80. Bourne, "Homelands," 22.

81. Ibid., 22.

CHAPTER FOUR

1. "Self-identification" poorly describes how group affiliations to a movement operate. Here I draw on Verta Taylor and Leila J. Rupp's important methodological distinction between ways of studying feminism. The first way posits an amorphous grouping of "a wide variety of struggles to improve women's inferior conditions as part of the women's movement" and the second limits itself to "women's own self-identification in defining the boundaries of the movement," while it recognizes how those boundaries marked by "class, race, national, and ethnic composition shaped its definition of interests and goals, recruitment strategies, levels of commitment, and mobilized resources." Verta Taylor and Leila J. Rupp, "Lesbian Existence and the Women's Movement," in *Feminism and Social Change,* ed. Heidi Gottfried (Urbana: University of Illinois Press, 1996), 145.

2. Gary Lehring, "Essentialism and the Political Articulation of Identity," in *Playing With Fire,* ed. Shane Phelan (New York: Routledge, 1997).

3. Martha Shelley, "Lesbianism and the Women's Liberation Movement," in *Women's Liberation: Blueprint for the Future,* ed. Sookie Stambler (New York: Ace Books, 1971), 124.

4. Shelley's inquiry into the relational instability of "lesbian" continues to lend insight into social commentary. For example, see Biddy Martin, "Sexual Practice and Changing Lesbian Identities," in *Femininity Played Straight: The Significance of Being Lesbian* (New York: Routledge, 1996). Urvaishi Vaid updates Shelley's contention for the present context: lesbian, she argues, is still more dangerous because of its association with feminism. Urvaishi Vaid, *Virtual Equality: The Mainstreaming of Gay and Lesbian Liberation* (New York: Anchor Books, 1995).

5. Many assessments of lesbian issues in feminism document continuing marginalization both of lesbians in feminist groups and of issues of lesbian sexuality. Their criticisms remind feminists that homophobia and heteronormativity are ongoing struggles with only incremental changes to show for it. These paradigmatic shifts are almost *despite* strong feminist resistance to lesbian sexuality as a feminist issue. See Taylor and Rupp, "Lesbian Existence," 149; Lisa Duggan and Nan D. Hunter, *Sex Wars: Sexual Dissent and Political Culture* (New York: Routledge, 1995), 158.

6. For an early criticism of homophobia within feminist demands for sexual autonomy, see Ti Grace Atkinson, *Amazon Odyssey* (New York: Links Books, 1974).

7. Barbara Ryan, *Feminism and the Women's Movement* (New York: Routledge, 1992), 44; Jo Freeman, *The Politics of Women's Liberation* (New York: David McKay, 1975), 99; Maren Lockwood Carden, *The New Feminist Movement* (New York: Russell Sage Foundation, 1974), 53–54.

8. Barry D. Adam, *The Rise of a Gay and Lesbian Movement* (Boston: Twayne, 1987), 91–92; Carden, *The New Feminist Movement,* 113–14.

9. Lehring, "Political Articulation of Identity," 174; Ruth Rosen, *The World Split Open: How the Modern Women's Movement Changed America* (New York: Viking Press, 2000), 174–45.

10. Seattle Radical Women, "Program and Structure" (October 1969), 5, Radical Women, Box 1, Acc. 1774, Manuscripts and University Archives Division, Univeristy of Washington, Seattle, WA; Kathy McAfee and Myrna Wood, "Bread and Roses," in *From Feminism to Liberation,* ed. Edith Hoshino Altbach, (Cambridge: Schenkman, 1971), 21–38. The article was first published in *Leviathan* 1:3 (June 1969).

11. Radicalesbians, "The Woman-Identified Woman," *Come Out!* (December 1970–January 1971), quoted in Donn Teal, *The Gay Militants* (New York: Stein and Day, 1971), 183–84.

12. Barry D. Adam, *Rise of a Gay and Lesbian Movement;* Susan Brownmiller, *In Our Time: Memoir of a Revolution* (New York: The Dial Press, 1999); John D'Emilio, *Sexual Politics, Sexual Communities* (Chicago: University of Chicago Press, 1983); Martin Duberman, *Stonewall* (New York: Plume, 1994); Alice Echols, *Daring to Be Bad: Radical Feminism in America 1967–1975* (Minneapolis: University of Minnesota Press, 1987); Karla Jay, *Tales of the Lavender Menace: A Memoir of Liberation* (New York: Basic Books, 1999).

13. Karla Jay and Allen Young, *Out of the Closets: Voices of Gay Liberation* (New York: New York University Press, 1992); Teal, *The Gay Militants.*

14. Anne Koedt, "The Myth of the Vaginal Organism," in *Radical Feminism,* ed. Anne Koedt, Ellen Levine, and Anita Rapone (New York: Quadrangle Books, 1973).

15. Koedt, "Myth," 206

16. Adam, *Rise of a Gay and Lesbian Movement,* 90; Sidney Abbott and Barbara Love, "Is Women's Liberation a Lesbian Plot?" in *Women in Sexist Society,* ed. Vivian Gornick and Barbara K. Moran (New York: Basic Books, 1971), 614.

17. Echols, *Daring to Be Bad,* 146.

18. Jay, *Lavender Menace,* 140.

19. Susan Brownmiller, "'Sisterhood Is Powerful': A Member of the Women's Liberation Movement Explains Its Aims," *New York Times Magazine* (15 March 1970), 140.

20. Echols, *Daring to Be Bad,* 215–17; Jay, *Lavender Menace,* 141–42.

21. Redstockings, "Redstockings Manifesto," in *Sisterhood Is Powerful* ed. Robin Morgan (New York: Random House, 1970), 535.

22. *Liberation Now! Writings from the Women's Liberation Movement* (New York: Dell, 1971), 292.

23. Ibid., 288.

24. Echols, *Daring to Be Bad,* 227. For a similar assessment, see Ryan, *Feminism and the Women's Movement,* 50.

25. Shane Phelan writes about the militance of lesbian separatist communities through their absolute rejection of differences among group members. Shane Phelan, *Getting Specific: Post-Modern Lesbian Politics* (Minneapolis: University of Minnesota Press, 1995), 16.

26. Cited in *The Gay Militants,* Teal, 186.

27. NOW National Task Force on Sexuality and Lesbianism, "The Newsletter on Sexuality and Lesbianism," Sidney Abbott Papers, Box 1, Sophia Smith Collection, Smith College, Northampton, MA. A telling handwritten note on the newsletter signed by Abbott states, "Frankly—I did the work to get this approved and going—made Betty Friedan livid."

28. Ibid., 5.

29. Sidney Abbott and Barbara Love, *Sappho was a Right-On Woman* (New York: Stein and Day, 1972), 134.

30. Freeman, *Politics of Women's Liberation,* 100.

31. Cited in Carden, *The New Feminist Movement,* 113, from "Resolutions of the 1971 Conference," in "Revolution: From the Doll's House to the White House!" (report presented at the Fifth Annual Conference of the National Organization for Women (NOW), Los Angeles, Calif., September 3–6, 1971, 16.

32. Myra Marx Ferree and Beth B. Hess portray the contours of lesbian sexuality as a single issue in NOW through the discourse of discrimination. Unfortunately, their characterization throughout their history suggests that lesbian sexuality functioned only as a single issue within feminism. Myra Marx Ferree and Beth B. Hess, *Controversy and Coalition: The New Feminist Movement* (Boston: Twayne, 1985), 104–5, 111, 160.

33. Sheila Tobias, "Feminism and Sexual Preference," in *Faces of Feminism* (Boulder, CO: Westview Press, 1997), 155–69; Dana R. Shugar, *Sep-a-ra-tism and Women's Community* (Lincoln: University of Nebraska Press, 1995), 33–34.

34. Echols's history suggests that the politics of alliance and coalition preceded that of separatism in lesbian feminism through her focus on such high-profile characters and groups as Rita Mae Brown and the Furies. These arguments may have gained ascendancy or public recognition in this historical progression, but also coexisted between 1969 and 1971. Echols, *Daring to Be Bad,* 213–32.

35. "Joan Comedy speech" Washington, D.C., (August 26, 1970), Charlotte Bunch Papers, Carton 2, Schlesinger Library, Radcliffe College, Cambridge, MA.

36. No title (May, 1971), Charlotte Bunch Papers, Carton 1, File 5, Schlesinger Library, Radcliffe College, Cambridge, MA.

37. Radicalesbians (New York City), "Leaving the Gay Men Behind," in *Out of the Closets,* ed. Jay and Young, 290.

38. Ibid., 292.

39. "Notes on Dyke Separatism" (n.d.), Noel Phyllis Birkby Papers, Box 36, Sophia Smith Collection, Smith College, Northampton, MA.

40. Ibid., 2.

41. Flora Davis, *Moving the Mountain: The Women's Movement in America since 1960* (Urbana: University of Illinois Press, 1999), 270–71.

42. Shane Phelan, *Identity Politics: Lesbian Feminism and the Limits of Community* (Philadelphia: Temple University Press, 1989).

43. For a thorough and often compelling refutation of this characterization, see Shugar's detailed study of lesbian separatism, *Sep-a-ra-tism and Women's Community.*

44. Davis cites one Bread and Roses member who recalled her reaction when lesbian sexuality emerged as an issue in Boston, but does not follow up on her memories of unease

for the whole group or women's movement in the city. Davis, *Moving the Mountain,* 269–70.

45. Seattle Radical Women, "Program and Structure," 5.

46. "Radical Women Program and Structure" (conference draft, March 1972), Melba Windoffer Papers, Box 2, University of Washington, Seattle, WA.

47. Ibid., 7.

48. Dorothy Chambless, "Race and Sex, 1972: Collision or Comradeship?" Women's Ephemera Files, Socioeconomic Theories—Papers, Folder 2, Northwestern University, Chicago, IL.

49. Seattle Radical Women, "Sexual Politics: Socialism and Emancipation of Women," *University of Washington Daily,* 16 May 1974.

50. McAfee and Wood, "Bread and Roses" 35.

51. "Women's Liberation Movement Course—Forum Series" (Spring 1970), Charlotte Bunch Papers, Carton 2, Schlesinger Library, Radcliffe College, Cambridge, MA.

52. "Bread and Roses Conference," Charlotte Bunch Papers, Carton 1, Folder 5, Schlesinger Library, Radcliffe College, Cambridge, MA.

53. Ibid.

54. Ibid.

55. Ibid.

56. Bernice Johnson Reagon, "Coalition Politics: Turning the Century," in *Home Girls: A Black Feminist Anthology,* ed. Barbara Smith (New York: Kitchen Table Women of Color Press, 1983), 356.

57. Biddy Martin and Chandra Talpade Mohanty, "Feminist Politics: What's Home Got to Do with It?" in *Feminity Played Straight,* ed. Martin, 163–84.

CHAPTER FIVE

1. Seyla Benhabib, "Feminism and Postmodernism," in *Feminist Contentions,* ed. Seyla Benhabib, Judith Butler, Drucilla Cornell, and Nancy Fraser (New York: Routledge, 1995), 24.

2. Johanna Brenner characterizes the two sides of feminism in the U.S., one of breaking barriers in management and the academy, the other both of worsening poverty for households headed by women and of eroding reproductive rights. This disparity plays out along strikingly parallel lines for theory versus activism. Feminist theory is alive and kicking, but feminist activism is nominal. Johanna Brenner, "The Best of Times, The Worst of Times: US Feminism Today," *New Left Review* (July–August 1993): 101–59.

3. *Struggle* contains implications of what Lewis Gordon calls instrumental activity and consensus building. He defines instrumental activity as "primarily functional and administrative," and consensus building as "matters of speech and agreement." Unorganized struggle, disconnected from a political movement, refers to the ongoing efforts of daily survival. Lewis Gordon, "Foreword," in *Transcending the Talented Tenth: Black Leaders and American Intellectuals,* Joy James (New York: Routledge, 1997), xiv.

4. Martin Luther King, "Our Struggle" in *A Documentary History of the Negro People in the United States,* vol. 6, ed. Herbert Aptheker (New York: Citadel Press Book, 1993), 330–36.

5. King, "Our Struggle," 333.

6. Margaret Benston, "The Political Economy of Women's Liberation," in *From Feminism to Liberation,* ed. Edith Hoshino Altbach (Boston: Schenkman, 1970), 199–210. The article was first published in the January 1969 issue of *Monthly Review.*

7. Christina Hoff Sommers, *Who Stole Feminism?* (New York: Simon and Schuster, 1994); Daphne Patai and Noretta Koertge, *Professing Feminism: Cautionary Tales from the Strange World of Women's Studies* (New York: Basic Books, 1995).

8. Naomi Wolf, *Fire with Fire: The New Female Power and How It Will Change the Twenty-First Century* (New York: Random House, 1993).

9. Judith Butler, "Merely Cultural," *Social Text* 15:3–4 (Fall-Winter 1997): 265–76.

10. Teresa Ebert, *Ludic Feminism and After* (Ann Arbor: University of Michigan Press, 1996).

11. Patricia Huntington, *Ecstatic Subjects, Utopia, and Recognition* (Albany: State University of New York, 1998); Kathi Weeks, *Constructing Feminist Subjects* (Ithaca: Cornell University Press, 1998).

12. Huntington, *Ecstatic Subjects, Utopia, and Recognition,* 83.

13. Linda Alcoff, "Cultural Feminism Versus Post-Structuralism: The Identity Crisis in Feminist Theory," *Signs* 13:3 (1988): 405–36.

14. Eric Alterman, "Making One and One Equal Two," *The Nation* 266:19 (25 May 1998): 10–11; Todd Gitlin, *The Twilight of Common Dreams: Why America is Wracked by Culture Wars* (New York: H. Holt, 1995); Richard Rorty, *Achieving Our Country* (Cambridge: Harvard University Press, 1998).

15. Karen Lehrman, "Off Course," *Mother Jones* 18:3 (September/October 1993): 45–51, 62, 64, 68; Alan Wolfe, "The Gender Question," *The New Republic* 4:142 (6 June 1994): 27–34. For a much less cursory analysis of right-wing feminist arguments, see Elizabeth Kamarck Minnich, "Feminist attacks of feminisms: Patriarchy's prodigal daughters," *Feminist Studies* 24:1 (Spring 1998): 159–75.

16. Christine Hoff Sommers, "On the Other Hand," *The American Enterprise* (Jan/Feb 1998): 57.

17. Todd Gitlin, "Organizing Across Boundaries," *Dissent* 44:4 (Fall 1997): 38–40.

18. Sommers, *Who Stole Feminism?,* 18.

19. Ibid.

20. Ibid., 22.

21. Ibid., 51.

22. Gitlin, "Organizing Across Boundries," 38.

23. Sara Evans's book, *Personal Politics,* provides careful historical research; the more contemporaneous essays by Robin Morgan, "Goodbye to All That," and Elinor Langer, "Notes for the Next Time," only scratch the surface of valuable accounts to aid an examination of the New Left's weaknesses in these struggles.

24. Butler, "Merely Cultural," 265.

25. Fraser's response to Butler highlights this inaccuracy regarding her own book, but this is equally a problem for commentators who side neither with the "class only" crowd, nor with Butler's argument. See Nancy Fraser, "Heterosexism, Misrecognition, and Capitalism: A Response to Judith Butler," *Social Text* 15:3–4 (Fall/Winter 1997): 279–83.

For a nonreductive position on class-based politics, see Adolph Reed, "Token Equality," *The Progressive* 61:2 (February 1997): 18–19.

26. Butler, "Merely Cultural," 269.

27. For an illuminating argument about identity and identity politics in relation to their institutionalization, see Wendy Brown, *States of Injury* (Princeton: Princeton University Press, 1995).

28. Butler, "Merely Cultural," 269.

29. Ibid., her emphasis.

30. Ebert, *Ludic Feminism and After,* 24.

31. Ibid., 37.

32. See chapter 1 for a definition of organization.

33. Ebert, *Ludic Feminism and After,*7.

34. Ibid., 10.

35. Ibid., 11.

36. Echols, *Daring to Be Bad: Radical Feminism in America, 1967–1975* (Minneapolis: Univeristy of Minnesota Press, 1987), 118.

37. Kwame Ture and Charles V. Hamilton, *Black Power: The Politics of Liberation* (New York: Vintage Books, 1992).

38. James Forman, *The Making of Black Revolutionaries* (Seattle: Open Hand, 1985), 450–51.

39. For example, see Robin Morgan, ed., *Sisterhood Is Powerful* (New York: Vintage Books, 1970), 520.

40. Echols, *Daring to Be Bad,* 103–37.

41. Sara Evans, *Personal Politics: The Roots of Women's Liberation in the Civil Rights Movement and the New Left* (New York: Knopf, 1979). See especially chapter 7, "The Failure of Success—Women in the Movement," and chapter 8, "The Dam Breaks."

42. Ellen Willis, "The Feminist Position," Jody Aliesan Papers, Acc. 2272, Box 12, Speeches and Writings, 1–3, Manuscripts and University Archives Division, Univeristy of Washington, Seattle, WA.

43. Beverly Jones and Judith Brown, "Toward a Female Liberation Movement" (Gainesville, FL,1968), 21, Social Action Vertical File, Box 58, Wisconsin State Historical Society (WSHS), Madison, WI.

44. Dana R. Shugar, *Sep-a-ra-tism and Women's Community* (Lincoln: University of Nebraska Press, 1995); Marge Piercy, "Grand Coolie Dam," *Leviathan* 6 (November 1969): 16–22.

45. Echols, *Daring to Be Bad,* 51–101.

46. Frances M. Beale, "Double Jeopardy: To be Black and Female" (ca. 1970), Women's Ephemera Files (WEF), Minority/Black Folder 1 Northwestern University (NU), Chicago, IL. Maryanne Weathers, "An Argument for Black Women's Liberation as a Revolutionary Force," Social Action Vertical File, Box 6, WSHS, Madison, WI.

47. "Third World Women's Alliance (Bay Area Chapter)" (n.d.), Pam Allen Papers, Box 4, WSHS, Madison, WI.

48. Their letters, beginning in 1966, are collected in the Joan Jordan Papers, WSHS, Madison, WI.

49. Other examples of groups who conceptualized the women's movement similarly are the Bay Area's Union W.A.G.E. for working women, and Women in Action in the New York City area.

50. Third World Women's Alliance, "Women in the Struggle," Melba Windoffer, Black Papers, Acc. 1798–2 Box 2, Manuscripts and University Archives, University of Washington, Seattle, WA. The Third World Women's Alliance developed from SNCC's women's caucus; the group's immediate predecessor was called Black and Third World Women's Liberation Alliance. The article was first published in *National SNCC Monthly* 1:6 (March 1971): 8.

51. Ibid., 5.

52. Joreen, "What in the Hell Is Women's Liberation Anyway?" *Voice of the Women's Liberation Movement* 1:1 (March 1968), 1, 4.

53. Beale, "Double Jeopardy," 2.

54. Weathers, "An Argument," 1.

55. Patricia Robinson to Joan Jordan (18 September 1969), Joan Jordan Papers, Box 2, WSHS, Madison, WI.

56. Joan Jordan Papers, Box 2, WSHS. The signatures and occupations of Women in Action members close the letter. A typed collection includes an article by Patricia Robinson entitled "Poor Black Women," Social Action Vertical Files, Box 40, WSHS.

57. Joyce Hoyt, Rita Van Lew, and Priscilla Leake to Margaret Benston (4 November 1968), Joan Jordan Papers, Box 2, WSHS.

58. Robinson to Jordan (1969).

59. Katie King suggests that this preoccupation with autonomy has led to the historiographic erasure of black women's groups and black feminists—a process which centered white women's political organization. She questions Echols's description of the 1968 Sandy Springs conference in light of this erasure and asks whether "a black feminist movement must be *autonomous* to count." Katie King, *Theory in its Feminist Travels: Conversations in U.S. Women's Movements* (Bloomington: Indiana University Press, 1994), 20–22.

60. Robinson to Jordan (1969).

61. Ibid.

62. For a similar conclusion written several years later, see Charlotte Bunch and Nancy Myron, eds., *Class and Feminism* (Baltimore, MD: Diana Press, 1974). See in particular Coletta Reid and Charlotte Bunch's essay in that collection, "Revolution Begins at Home."

63. Echols, *Daring to Be Bad,* 106–7.

64. Clara Colon, in the Communist Party USA's book on women's liberation, argued that working-class, black, and Native American women should lead the trade union movement and anti-imperialist movements to greater militancy. See Clara Colon, *Enter Fighting: Today's Woman, a Marxist-Leninist View* (New York: New Outlook, 1970), 9, 27.

65. Jordan to Robinson (1967), Joan Jordan Papers, Box 2, WSHS.

66. Ibid.

67. Like Beale, Jordan draws from an earlier essay by Communist Party USA member Claudia Jones that propounds similar views about leadership by black women in the union movement and within left parties. Claudia Jones, "An End to the Neglect of Negro Women!" *Political Affairs* (June 1949). Rebecca Hill historicizes Jones's essay in relation to

the Cold War and the second wave women's movement. Rebecca Hill, "Fosterites and Feminists, or 1950s Ultra-Leftists and the Invention of AmeriKKKa," *New Left Review* 228 (March/April 1998): 67–90.

CONCLUSION

1. Rosalyn Baxandall and Linda Gordon, "Second-Wave Soundings," *The Nation* 271:1 (July 3, 2000): 28–32.

2. Baxandall and Gordon charge recent histories and biographies with focusing on "sexual issues," but as the materials from chapter 4 show, sexual issues in the second wave women's movement are shot through with radical and revolutionary aspirations. Ibid., 31.

3. Inderpal Grewal and Caren Kaplan, "Introduction," in *Scattered Hegemonies* ed. Grewal and Kaplan (Minneapolis: University of Minnesota Press, 1944), 20.

Manuscript Collections

University of California at Berkeley, Berkeley, California
    Bancroft Library, Social Protest Collection

Center for Socialist History, Berkeley, California
    Social Action Files
    Women's Movement
    Miscellaneous flyers and folders

Holt Labor Library, New College of California, San Francisco, California
    Labor Unions
    Socialist Workers Party

Meiklejohn Civil Liberties Institute, Berkeley, California

Newsreel Movies, San Francisco, California
    Women's Movement films and publications

Niebyl-Proctor Marxist Library for Social Research, Berkeley, California
    Angela Davis
    Feminism
    Women and Labor Unions

Northwestern University Library, Evanston, Illinois
    Special Collections Department, Women's Collection
    Women's Ephemera File

Reference Center for Marxist Studies, New York City, New York
    Claudia Jones
    Communist Party
    Young Communist League

San Francisco State University, San Francisco, California
    Coalition of Labor Union Women
    Ann Draper
    Special Collections
    Union W.A.G.E.

Arthur and Elizabeth Schlesinger Library on the History of Women in America, Radcliffe College, Cambridge, Massachusetts
    Women's Liberation Files
    Charlotte Bunch

Sophia Smith Collection, Smith College, Northhampton, Massachusetts
    Sidney Abbott
    Noel P. Birkby
    Lisa Leghorn
    Women's Action Alliance

Manuscripts and University Archives, University of Washington, Seattle, Washington
    Clara Fraser
    Mary Gibson
    Socialist Workers Party
    Students for a Democratic Society
    Melba Windoffer

Archives Division, University of Wisconsin State Historical Society, Madison, Wisconsin
    Pam Allen papers
    Radical America papers
    Social Action Vertical Files

INDEX

K20136.